super
frank

frank lampard

Douglas Thompson

super frank

frank lampard

JOHN BLAKE

Published by John Blake Publishing Ltd,
3, Bramber Court, 2 Bramber Road,
London W14 9PB, England

www.blake.co.uk

This edition first published in paperback in 2006

ISBN 1 84454 254 8

British Library Cataloguing-in-Publication Data:

A catalogue record for this book is available from the British Library.

Design by www.envydesign.co.uk

Printed in Great Britain by Bookmarque

1 3 5 7 9 10 8 6 4 2

Pictures reproduced by kind permission of All Action, Clevamedia, Empics,
Getty Images and Mirrorpix and John Ingledew (prints of John Ingledew's
photographs are available from www.chelseabluesinblackandwhite.com)

Every attempt has been made to contact the relevant copyright holders,
but some were unobtainable. We would be grateful if the appropriate people
could contact us.

Papers used by John Blake Publishing are natural, recyclable products
made from wood grown in sustainable forests. The manufacturing processes
conform to the environmental regulations of the country of origin.

In memory, Ross Benson, Chelsea evenings,
California days.

Acknowledgements

It's a privilege to have so many talented friends and I thank all of them who have helped me tell the inspirational and exciting story of the superb talent that is Frank Lampard Junior. He's an England star of now and of the future with a host of accolades and honours to his name, including being named, in 2005, as Player of the Year in a Football Association poll.

He is a great ambassador for both football and his country, a relentless ingredient of Chelsea's magnificent resurgent and recurring success, all of which was lucky for me as everyone has an opinion about him. And football people like to tell you what they think. To list all who have helped with interviews and analysis would take another book, but I'd like to thank the renowned sports broadcaster Guy Swindells, who has chronicled Frank's career from the beginning, for his insight and time.

And all those in Romford, Canning Town, Barking and

Stratford, Manchester, Leeds, Edinburgh, Glasgow, Italy, Portugal, Spain and America for their indulgence.

Bobby Moore's close friend and authorised biographer, Jeff Powell, has witnessed much more of this overlapping tale than most and was kind enough to offer me some of his wisdom. Jon Ryan, an ongoing source of discernment in the media arena, was, as he has been for what turns out to be a rather disquieting number of years, a good friend and a tremendous help.

All those who illustrated the early days of Frank Senior – their hairstyles may have changed or vanished but their diligence and attitude has not. I also owe huge thanks to John Hiscock, the distinguished graduate from the *Chelsea News*, Maggie May for the comprehensive sporting education at the Markham Arms, and most especially two other sisters from Barking for their insight and memories.

Salutations.

Contents

PART TWO
The Blues

'There is a saying in Italy that you do not sell the bear's skin until you have shot it.'

CLAUDIO RANIERI

'Frank is definitely one of the best players in the world. Not just because he is my player, even before that.'

JOSE MOURINHO, 18 SEPTEMBER 2004

'Frank Lampard is a very important player, the complete midfielder, because he can defend, he's a good tackler, good passer and scores goals. You can't ask much more of a midfielder.'

ENGLAND MANAGER SVEN-GORAN ERIKSSON,
20 JANUARY 2005

'Frank Lampard is a future England captain, no doubt.'

KEVIN KEEGAN, 1998

'The fans know who they love. And they love winners. They love the truth. They love Frank – you can't cheat the fans. They know. They *always know.*'

CLAUDIO RANIERI, FEBRUARY 2005

'He is our best player.'

CHELSEA FC OWNER, ROMAN ABRAMOVICH, JANUARY 2005

'We're determined to be in Germany for the World Cup in 2006.'

FRANK LAMPARD JUNIOR, JANUARY 2005

'Frank Lampard is a player every manager would like to have.'

SVEN-GORAN ERIKSSON, JULY 2005

'Frank Lampard has been on fire in the last couple of years.'

JAMIE CARRAGHER, JULY 2005

'Frank is Chelsea's important player – bombing forward and getting in the box.'

STEVEN GERRARD, OCTOBER 2005

'Frank Lampard is outstanding. He's got great World Cup goal potential.'

TERRY VENABLES, OCTOBER 2005

'Lampard is exceptional. He can take on any role asked of him.'

DIEGO MARADONA, OCTOBER 2005

'He's the best in the world.'

'Frank is a great penalty-taker, so him doing the job is
better for the team.'

'Frank Lampard has been playing out of his skin.'

'I think he's probably the most effective player in the world.
He's different class, Frank.'

'What can we find wrong with him?'

'He's the one player who can get goals from anywhere.
He's the one who can come up with magic.'

'I admire Frank enormously. He is so very, very good.'

Preface

'Lampard, Lampard, Lampard!!!
Super Frankie Lampard!!!!'

THE CHELSEA CROWD CHANTING CHORUSES BEFORE THE
KICK-OFF AT STAMFORD BRIDGE, 26 DECEMBER 2004

It seems only a moment ago that the fashionable fragment of the football world, the chic and the cheeky side that made mischief personally and professionally, which sought and got most attention, flaunted itself and swaggered along the King's Road.

Then, for a time, it became more of a stagger on that singular London thoroughfare. It was suddenly smarter to be far more pragmatic about the advertising budget; there was not much to show off.

Now, some long years on, there's that satisfying bounce of self-confidence, of propriety and dignity both in and about the vicinity. The billboards are back to shout the 21st-century attitude. Chelsea Football Club are once again charismatic champions in the game and the Blues are where fashion and football connect; it might not be as painfully trendy as the sixties, but once again on a sunny

SUPER FRANK

Saturday afternoon it can appear, through the Persol sunglasses, more St Tropez than the west side of London.

It's a place where David Beckham would be comfortable with the lads from Real Madrid. Certainly, Chelsea's image-conscious imported players are. Ken Bates never tired of pointing out that by the Louis Vuitton route, by taxi, it's only ten minutes from Stamford Bridge to Harrods where you can buy just about anything.

Yet, for two decades, the bearded, ebullient, but financially coy, Bates was where the buck stopped at the Bridge. And, of course, Roman Abramovich, who took over from him in 2003 as the club's ultimate boss, is where the bucks started.

The enigmatic Abramovich changed the rules on retail therapy for football clubs around the world. He warmed up the finances of football by spending more than £100 million in exchange for eleven players in half-a-dozen weeks.

By the beginning of 2005 that spending spree had grown, in those neat round numbers we all like, to more than £250 million.

With all that simmering, oil-soaked currency, dollars, euros, sterling, it was a convincing thought that world football would be better equipped with chancellors than with coaches. It seemed that the Bank of England might have to change interest rates if Chelsea fancied a new goalkeeper and a couple of strikers in the same weekend. It still does.

Amid all that frenzy and speculation, where did the Chelsea football team stand in that summer and autumn of 2003? Initially, they were as perplexed and puzzled as weekend whist players caught up in the World Poker Championships.

How big's the pot? The odds? What's the betting? Who plays? Who goes? Who stays? And, of course, who is in charge?

The genial Claudio Ranieri, who took Chelsea to second in the Premiership and the semi-final of the Champions League before succumbing a few months later to the biggest peril in football – events – got extra time.

He believes that was by happenstance, which, of course, is just events in disguise, 'When the new owner arrived, I thought he'd change everything, the manager first. But Sven-Goran Eriksson was not available, so Roman gave me the opportunity to drive the new car. But I knew Roman didn't want me to drive the car, he wanted Schumacher...'

Uncertain times. Just what could the Russian oil billionaire's financial power do? And, more importantly, for young Frank Lampard, who would it buy? Or sell? What had the lad from the East End with West End ambitions landed in?

It wasn't Abramovich's millions which bought him on 14 June 2001 for £11 million from West Ham and took him up west. Then, he still had demons to exorcise, mental and physical strengths to improve, disciplines to learn.

Two summers later what he required more than anything was 100 per cent self-belief. It was difficult. And, without it, the cheque-book football going on around him made him frightened for his future with Chelsea. He thought he would be on the bench, as glamour names were bought in from around the globe. He firmly believed he would be squeezed out of the team.

Incredible as it seems, with hindsight, Frank Lampard thought he had a no-hope future at Chelsea. And, if so, what of his England dreams? He'd been an England Under-21 captain and for years they'd been telling him that one day he would lead his national squad to grown-up glory.

'The worst feeling was seeing the extent of the speculation. You'd be reading about five defenders, five midfielders, five attackers, all being linked with Chelsea every day. I think you're entitled to feel unsettled when all that's raging around you. It would be unnatural not to. You've got to be allowed to think, Blimey, is somebody going to come in and take my position away?'

His instincts and training kicked in: he confronted the challenge. It wasn't in his brave and bold nature not to. Frank took up the gauntlet. 'I wanted to have a big season. I wanted to have the best season I'd ever had. I wanted to be part of the new Real Madrid. And I had a chance to show I could be part of it. That's what it was and I wanted to be involved with that. The situation at Chelsea was the sweetest dream as a footballer. I wanted to be playing in the Champions League final. I wanted to win the Premiership. There is so much belief in this squad that we believe we can win everything.'

And he was willing to work overtime to achieve the expectations that belief dictated.

He was brought up in the traditional English football

family, in the pre-Starbucks old school where managers passionately talked tactics with their players over suspect bacon and eggs in greasy cafes, the HP sauce bottle and the salt and pepper pots part of the 'war games', the Heinz ketchup and teacups defending, the forks and knives and spoons in attack formation, the sticky Colman's mustard jar the inside post.

It had been his father Frank Lampard's classroom during his many years with West Ham and there were lots of hard knocks in the lessons, on and off the field.

The attitude back then was that, even if you were injured, you played on; you got on with it. Then you got up and did it all over again. You played every game you possibly could. You embraced the pain.

His father learned by watching and listening to Bobby Moore representing England and playing for West Ham. The always perfectly calm Moore rated Frank Senior extremely highly; the work ethic, the training, the extra training, was passed on from the only England captain to lead his country to a World Cup win to his friend and team-mate.

That, in turn, was passed on from father to son: the two Frank Lampards mirror each other in more than name.

When Ron Greenwood wrote of the much-missed Bobby Moore in his autobiography *Yours Sincerely*, he might well have been writing about the Frank Lampard of 2005, a player who has the capacity to emulate Moore with the national team: 'He read the game uncannily well, his anticipation always seemed to give him a head start, he was icily cold at moments of high stress and his positional sense was impeccable. He was at his best when his best was most needed and his concentration never let up. He made football look a simple and lovely art.'

It was in this world that young Frank paid attention. He learned his lessons at his father's often black and blue, bruised knees.

Which is why he thrived at the nervy centre of Chelsea's spend, spend, spend culture. He did what he did best – his work. He got on with his job in an extraordinary atmosphere and didn't just survive but thrived during Chelsea's remarkable metamorphis from bankrupt to bankrolled.

Terry Venables, who has the Chelsea captaincy on his colourful CV, said in 2004 that no one 'in their wildest dreams' could have predicted the 'extraordinary chain of events that has made Chelsea the most talked-about football club in the world today'.

Certainly, before Abramovich moved his sporting interests to the West, Chelsea were facing fantastic debts, showing losses rivalled only by Fulham and Leeds. The talk was not of championships and Europe, but of survival. What if Abramovich hadn't materialised?

In early 2003 Chelsea were not the most obvious choice. Abramovich wanted a team in the Champions League. It did not look like Frank and his team-mates would make it.

The big hurdle, the last game of the season, was against Liverpool at the Bridge on 11 May 2003. Just under 42,000 people turned up to see Frank and the Blues triumph 2–1.

It was more than another victory: for on that day that

line-up of numbers was enough to win them the football lottery.

Russian Revolution? History! In football terms, Abramovich's purchase of Chelsea was a much bigger shake-up. Yet, Frank Lampard had learned *his* history lessons, with his A-grade Latin. He became one of Chelsea's highest-class performers, one of English football's top-three earners (on £99,000 a week in early 2005) and regularly the fulcrum of the team.

Frank Lampard introduced his own grammar into the Babel of world football. It was distinctive and winning. The player who believed he might be locked out of the squad instead became its lynchpin, a leader and an inspiration. He's now as requisite, as indispensable as it ever gets in one of the most dispensable businesses where, at his level, a hamstring is about all you've got between yourself and a multi-million-pound career.

One reason was because Frank was always playing, always on the field. His record of more than 130 consecutive appearances provoked Sir Alex Ferguson to pronounce Frank's feat as 'freakish'.

A strange choice of word. Then again, the fiercely competitive Ferguson would hire Frankenstein and the bearded lady if they had Frank's talent with a football. Rival fans, of course, would say Ferguson already has one or two.

'I always want to play and there are a few reasons I can. One has to be luck, not getting injured. Another is I play with minor knocks at times. I'm not saying I'm Braveheart compared to others, but I do just get on with it. And I do a lot of extra work; not so much gym work, I won't go in and pump iron, but I do like to do as much as I can on the training pitch. I'll practise my finishing, my passing, my dribbling and my sprints. Maybe that all contributes to that bit of luck I have staying fit. It's something my old man has instilled in me since I was a kid. Now, if I don't do that bit extra, I don't go into the game feeling I've prepared right.'

His strict regimen has paid off. His is one of the first names on an England teamsheet. His ever-present performance in Euro 2004 was overshadowed by the emergence of Wayne Rooney, but that was in the media spotlight, not in the dressing and conference rooms of world football. Rooney was a super story. Lampard was already a great, established player.

Months on, in January 2005, that was accepted fact and Frank got 40 per cent of the vote as Footballer of the Year for 2004. England captain David Beckham – the winner in 2003 – was in sixth place. Wayne Rooney was second (16 per cent) followed by Steven Gerrard (9.8), Ashley Cole (9.4) and Shaun Wright-Phillips (7).

'I wouldn't say it's fair, that's not my job,' England coach Sven-Goran Eriksson said diplomatically. But, still careful with his words, he added, 'I congratulate Frank who has done very well for us.'

Frank is a champion, a Footballer of the Year, a graduate of a tough but honest, solid and loyal background and upbringing, and considered by the experts as the most effective midfielder in English football. They say the boy is the father of the man.

PREFACE

As such, with a childhood smothered in England football legend, Frank Lampard Junior has an extravagant pedigree. He is employed by one of the youngest, all-around thoroughly, dutifully controversial, and richest men in the world. He is looking at huge honours for his club and country and personally.

Chelsea are celebrated as the most entertaining team in England in their centenary year of 2005. They are enormous on the world stage – their kit is now sold in 90 countries and Frank's No. 8 jersey is a favourite world-wide. It sells in Beijing as well as Barking.

On the horizon, forty years on from that other East End boy Bobby Moore's global conquest, is World Cup 2006.

Anything is possible, especially in such a landmark year. At the centre of it is Frank Lampard. He's known from television to the terraces as 'Lamps', but with such a worldwide buzz he deserves another title. Let's call him the Prince of the King's Road.

Christmas Day in the Workhouse

'Everyone is selected.'

JOSE MOURINHO,
23 DECEMBER 2004

It is extraordinary that, for such a solid, circumspect Englishman, Frank Lampard's immediate past and future are entangled with the more emotional, much beloved and often eccentric Claudio Ranieri and the modern, upfront, straight-talking, no-nonsense Jose Mourinho: the ying and yang of European mentality. It also seems extraordinary that he has flourished both as a man and a player under the influence of both men.

But Frank's greatest strength is that he will learn from anyone who has something worthwhile to teach him. His well-brought-up manners dictate that he will give anyone the time of day. His skill is to remember what matters.

'I feel like Michelangelo. If the marble is good I can improve the player,' said Claudio Ranieri. And he added, with pride, 'I like to think I improved Frank Lampard.'

Mourinho is simpler, 'I love Frank Lampard. I want to make him a better player.'

And Frank himself has learned much from the two managers' styles. Ranieri's tactics were of the moment, often orgulous; everything Mourinho dictates is pre-planned, deeply thought out, Machiavellian. Frank is diplomatic, for he holds great admiration and fondness for Ranieri. 'First and foremost Claudio is a good man and that's the most important thing.

'Maybe the tinkering didn't always pay off, but I couldn't have more respect for him. I was with England when he left Chelsea but I phoned him and thanked him for everything he did. He helped me a lot. Now, it's Jose and he's helped me a lot, too.'

He knows he has become a more powerful personality and player with his present boss. Mourinho is round-the-clock motivated – he's brought a more ruthless edge to Chelsea. And to Frank.

'The mental attitude now is win, win, win. Jose is a pleasure to work with. He's always working on your position in the team. If you're in a keep-ball session, he will want me in the middle as if it's a match. His training is precise.

'It wasn't like that so much before. Now the accent is on winning every game we play and every competition we are in.'

Which took Frank to Christmas in 2004 at the Bridge, which the record books show has not been a time for good cheer for the Chelsea team. They had not won a Boxing Day fixture for five years and only twice in fifteen years.

The opposition was Aston Villa, a useful side determined

not to be another notch on the Chelsea list, another tick on the Blues' clear drive to the Premiership title.

But Frank was chanting Chelsea's mantra: Win, win, win! There were no thoughts for the ghosts of Christmas Past.

And win they did, but by a whisper at 1–0. Damien Duff had the honour. Frank had wanted to be up front, but was forced to defend as the game was like most family Boxing Days, something of a mess, a bit of an embarrassment and lots of leftovers, and with everyone hoping that somebody would do the right thing. Frank did. He fed the ball through and it was passed on to Duff's feet. The Irishman then powered it inside the near post.

It tells much of Frank's story that he put the victory down to the team's discipline and hard work.

The only festive indication in Jose Mourinho's preparation for Aston Villa had been to allow his players to start training three hours later than normal on Christmas Day.

'At the moment I only have sixteen players and I cannot give anyone a day off. Everyone is selected. I need everybody. We don't have many midfield players at the moment.'

In Frank's world, Christmas is a time for the two things the Lampards hold most dear – family and football. What's important is being selected. And seeing the family. He did it all at Christmas in 2004.

'Christmas has always been dictated by football. I don't remember Dad as a player but as a coach. Christmas Day was always disrupted when he had to go off training. It's

3

my turn. I've done it for years as a player and I look upon it as normal. I went to my mum and dad's in Essex for the first part of the day. We had Christmas dinner – but it was nothing heavy for me because I had to be back at Cobham [Chelsea's superb training facility in Surrey] for early-evening training. I went back home and then off to Stamford Bridge and Aston Villa.'

His father would love to have his son at home for the whole day but totally understands. 'It was always that way. I can recall going back to my mum's house in Barking and having an early night before playing the following morning. That was the way it was. The groundwork was a big thing for Frank. You either had to get tough or get out. Frank got tough.

'Football is still very much part of my life. Watching Frank is an outlet for me. I'm very proud of him because, although I used to play, he's done it for himself.

'There was a newspaper story that, when some of the other Chelsea players went in at the end of training, Frank Lampard stayed out to do some laps. Now, that's a big thing for me. Bobby Moore used to do that. He used to pile on the sweat tops and go running after training – especially if he had been out the night before. Frank's learned that.

'I'm not as jittery as I used to be when I watch him play – and I see every match I can. I could see things in the game that Frank could have done better, but he's learned and I can't teach him much, to be honest, but I still chip in.

'He might have scored a great goal, but I want to talk to him about something else in the game where perhaps he could have done better. I thought Ranieri did a lot for Frank in terms of team situations. I thought he was a tremendous manager. Mourinho has taken them on again. He seems very methodical, leaves nothing to chance. You can see he has instilled the confidence he feels into his players. Frank has worked hard and learned well.'

And those are the words of the most involved mentor of Frank's life. Frank Senior – he and his wife Pat were in their usual seats at Stamford Bridge on Boxing Day – never wants to be accused of indulging or overpraising his son. Yet, he admits, 'He must be doing something right. The Chelsea fans chant his name before the kick-off. That's a big, big signal for me. You know why? You can't kid them.'

His son thrives on that encouragement – and on the disciplines of Jose Mourinho. 'He gets in early and is very organised. You know exactly what your day and whole week will involve. Each training session has a real purpose. That is spelled out at the beginning of the day.

'Training is intense with no time for slacking or relaxation. The joking comes afterwards. When Jose arrived there was a freshness about the place. We'd got a very exciting manager.

'People easily get the wrong impression of managers from the press. Ours has one attitude when he's speaking to the media and another with us. Yes, he can be strict, but he can also be matey in the way he chats to you.

'He'll have a joke and put an arm around you. He really cares about his players and treats us like his family.

'Manchester United and Real Madrid are the benchmark, having been successful over the past few years, but we're up there with them. With what we've got, the owner and a very exciting manager, why as a player would you want to go anywhere else?

'I joined Chelsea because I wanted to be challenging for honours. I knew that somebody was going to have to fight very, very hard if they wanted to take my place away. I was never going to give it up without a tough struggle. I am the man in possession.

'I think one of Jose's strengths is that he understands his players and their needs at any given time. He's very approachable. Right from the start I was comfortable with him and I think all of us felt that way. He gave me confidence by saying, "I want you to carry on, but I want to make you a better player."' But how?

Mourinho revealed, 'Frank can remain the same individually, but I wanted to change him in relation to the team.

'If one day I tell Frank I don't want him to be a box-to-box player but to hold back, he has to adapt to our needs. Wonderfully, he can.'

Mutual admiration: 'The manager is great at giving confidence. He has made me believe in myself even more.'

Yet, in the East End way, he'd been taught that almost from the day he was born – on 20 June 1978.

Part One
East End Roots

Chapter One
The Family Business

'He's destined for the very top. He's dedicated, he trains like a
demon, he's a great lad and he's got a great attitude.'

SOUTHAMPTON BOSS HARRY REDKNAPP TALKING IN 1998
ABOUT HIS NEPHEW FRANK LAMPARD

For much of the past century, London's East End was
patrolled by the valiant and the villains, but, whichever beliefs or trade were adhered to, the family always
came first.

Frank Lampard's upbringing, which had novel and
unorthodox aspects as he was to find out, was very much
meat and potatoes from the outset. It was traditional. Dad
was playing football. Or he was down the Black Lion pub,
sipping lager with Bobby Moore and the lads. His mother
Pat would be in the kitchen, and her sister Sandra's
husband Harry Redknapp, Uncle 'Arry, would be talking
about the future of West Ham with Frank Lampard Senior.
And, after that other bottle of red wine, predicting the
futures of the cousins, Frank Junior and his own son,
Jamie Redknapp.

What an England line-up! What a night out!

His dad was a Barking boy and Uncle Harry's local pub was the Blind Beggar in London's Whitechapel, where George Cornwell was murdered by the Kray twins, the bullet from Ronnie's gun and the urging from Reg Kray.

It was that sort of topsy-turvy world. Money, politics and football. What's changed?

'Appy 'Arry Redknapp and Frank Senior were heroes. They'd go to *Top of the Pops* and meet Pan's People and the Rolling Stones and The Who, but they'd rather be back in the East End at the Ilford Palais or the Room at the Top nightclub where they knew the words to the songs.

Football made them stars, not dockers.

Frank Lampard Senior began his career at West Ham in 1967 with World Cup heroes like Bobby Moore, Martin Peters and Geoff Hurst, the Boleyn Boys. He made 633 appearances for West Ham and played twice for his country.

He became part of East End football folklore when he played in West Ham's 1980 FA Cup final win over Arsenal. That victory only became possible because of his unheralded appearance in Everton's penalty area, when he scored a back-post header after a cross from Trevor Brooking, in the semi-final replay. OK, it was the defender's dance around the corner flag that contributed as much to his legend as the goal.

The one man he couldn't handle with a football was Harry Redknapp SENIOR.

A clever player, the elder Harry Redknapp confused the much younger man when they had a kick-around game on the Isle of Sheppey in the late 1970s. And Frank Senior had just been picked to play for England; his brother-in-law still enjoys telling the story.

The two men are from the fringes of London, only a couple of Tube stops from Upton Park. When Frank (born in Canning Town on 20 September 1948) and Harry (born in Poplar on 2 March 1947) met Pat and Sandra Harris, sisters from Barking, they didn't stretch their geographical expectations.

Silver Wedding anniversaries long ago celebrated, it seems the marriages were destined to be. Harry met Sandra and they went out for some time before breaking up.

Later, by chance, his fellow player Frank started going out with Pat Harris. And learned that her sister had once dated his pal Harry. Frank Senior takes up the story: 'I suppose I was to blame. We were both players, Harry and I, and when I started to go out with my wife, who was then called Pat Harris, she told me that her older sister, Sandra, used to go out with Harry. So I suggested a foursome, Harry and Sandra got together again and it ended up with both couples getting married.'

The West Ham boys romanced the two sisters where local highlights were once visits to Barking Baths. 'For weekend dances they used to floor over the swimming pool and have a band at the deep end,' recalled Patricia Brown, who worked on the local newspaper.

'You could smell the chlorine, but for lots of people in Barking and Romford and Ilford it was a big night out. There was nowhere else to go. The alternative was the Ilford Palais, but that was about it.

'Later, for Frank and Harry and the sisters, there would

11

be the Lotus Club in Stratford and also the boxer Billy Walker's club in Forest Gate.

'It was a different world: I'd see Bobby Moore, who was from Barking, on the 23C bus on his way to Upton Park. He'd get on at River Road.

'Today it's all Ferraris and private jets – back then one of England's greatest ever players took the bus. Pele was the world's greatest attacking footballer and Bobby was the world's great defender – and he'd be taking the 23C bus.

'Were they better days? I don't know.

'For us they were all major stars – Frank Lampard and Harry Redknapp were the youngsters following Bobby and Martin Peters and Geoff Hurst. West Ham was where it mattered and Frank and Harry kept it in the family.'

Frank Senior explained, 'It was all football when Frank was growing up. The family have been lifelong West Ham fans and it seemed inevitable that Frank would join the club. He had offers from Tottenham, but it was always the Hammers for him.'

Young Frank and his sisters – Claire was aged thirty-four and Natalie thirty in 2005 heard football stories, the dramas, the near-misses, the mistaken referees, the boneheaded management – and managers – and the egotistical players, the temperamental ones and the class acts; they lived the ups and downs of the glories and defeats.

Every Saturday, three hours before home games, Dad would eat a steak. Before 6pm, around the time *Dr Who* started and they'd finished reading the football pools results on the radio and television, Frank Senior would be in the Black Lion with Bobby Moore and the others after one whistle blew and a different tune started. The personnel may have changed, but the routine for Frank Senior didn't vary too much between 1967 and 1985.

'Most of us came from the same area and we were mates. We'd enjoy ourselves, but if you do the right things on the pitch I believe it helps make you lucky.

'Even when you pack up playing, the discipline which served you well as a player still holds you in good stead. We did a lot of long-distance running and we didn't see a ball for ten days. We had someone to help us with our agility work, but warm-ups took ten minutes then; now it's half an hour at least and it involves much more stretching.

'Bobby Moore used to come in on a Sunday morning after the night before. He would put on a tracksuit, a couple of jumpers and do ten laps around Upton Park.

'The biggest difference, though, is off the pitch. We could go out, have a few beers and relax, but now these players have to watch what they do.'

'Win or lose always on the booze' was Bobby Moore's saying, and one that was often repeated by Uncle Harry. Harry Redknapp made 149 League appearances for West Ham before moving to Bournemouth in 1972. His life at Upton Park, like many of his team-mates, revolved around the game, betting, on cards and the dogs, and enjoying a drink.

'We were just East End kids who went into football. That was the way it was in the sixties, but professional footballers can't do that any more. They have to be more aware of diet, training and how they behave.'

He's renowned for his quick often self-deprecating wit. 'Even when they had Moore, Hurst and Peters, West Ham's average finish was about 17th. It just shows how crap the other eight of us were.'

'When our family gets together, all we do is talk football. In the old days I'd go round my mum Violet's and have a cup of tea and egg and chips and a chat. And we'd watch the football. What more do you want?'

Harry Redknapp said of Bobby Moore in his auto-biography (Harper Collins, 1998), 'In my eyes he was every kid's hero. I have a picture of him and in it he's only ten years old, playing for Barking schoolboys.

'There he is, the team captain, the blonde locks flowing, collecting the trophy. Looking at it you can imagine he knew his destiny was to go on and captain his country and win the greatest trophy in the world.'

Frank Lampard Senior was born 'just down the road from the Boleyn' and was a players' player from the word go. He just frowns at any suggestion that he might have played for any other club than West Ham: 'Claret and blue flows through my blood.'

In 1971, Sir Alf Ramsey gave official recognition to his talents by naming him in the England Under-23 side. Originally spotted by the legendary scout Wally St Pier, the strong (5ft 10in, 12 stone in his day) defender had suffered a severe leg break in 1967 and endured a long and painful recovery; but for that his England career may have enjoyed more of a flourish.

'They were raising eyebrows about Frank's future after he broke his leg,' said an old friend of the player's in 2005.

'I went to visit when he came home from hospital. His mum, a very dejected lady, opened the door to me.

'He had a hip-length plaster on and was not a happy man. He had been done down. The leg was a major problem and he'd not heard much of anything from anybody. I had a chat and gave him some magazines along with lots of encouragement.

'I was just a friend. I had no influence in football, but I was concerned for him. He's been kind to me ever since, for many, many years. It's just the way he is. He's not a man to show emotion, but it's something that runs deep inside the Lampards. It's in his boy, too.

'Either of them would fight to the death for you if they believed in your cause. Or in you. Look at Frank's mam that day with the broken leg. Nobody at the club had gone to see him. Their attitude seemed to be: "The boy is finished – that's that." But his mum never forgot my visit. Every time I'd see her she'd rush up to me and give me a peppermint and a smile.'

Frank Senior has blocked much of the pain and frustration of that bust-up leg from his memory, but did reveal: 'If I have one regret, it is not winning more caps for my country. But the moment I walked on to Wembley in an England shirt was the proudest of my life. I've still got the shirt tucked away somewhere – it is a trophy they can never take away.

'The feeling of walking out in front of such a huge crowd is indescribable and one that stays with you forever. Things change when you represent your country. Wherever you go, fans want to shake your hand and talk to you…'

In 1973, Brian Clough was with Derby County and tried to buy Bobby Moore and Frank Senior from West Ham. 'Mr Clough was turned down flat,' the Hammers manager Ron Greenwood, in ailing health in early 2005, revealed at the time. It was great fuel for the lads' gossip, though.

Frank Senior took out insurance for his family's future by investing in the haulage business, a pub and a dry cleaners in Canning Town, but his first priority was always football.

He arrived at West Ham as the guard of Moore (who played 642 times for West Ham between 1958 and 1974), Hurst and Peters was beginning to change, 'The great strength of the sixties team was that it had its roots in that part of London.

'It was one of the few real areas of England which bred footballers and, in those days, it was always around them that West Ham's future lay. I would love to have had some of that sixties spirit in my teams.'

Frank Senior went on to say, 'I come from Canning Town. It is right on the doorstep for the club. In those days times were hard and one way out of it was to become a footballer. All my mates at school – all we wanted to be were footballers.

'I just felt I had done all right and that football had given me a chance to experience things and places I wouldn't have been able to do otherwise in life.

'I thought that if Frank was good enough to come through as a player then the rewards are there.

'I don't think I am any different from any other dad in that I am my son's worst critic and yet his biggest punter.

It's not been easy for him to make the grade, as he's had to put up with the sniping behind his back.

'I always stressed to Frank that he should be more of an attacking player, because it is always the midfielders and the strikers who get all the accolades.

'When I was a kid Bobby Moore was one of my heroes. The way I played, the way I thought about the game was from him.'

Moore, only fifty-one years old when he died from colon cancer in February 1993, had offered his thoughts on the training and encouragement of young stars like Frank Junior in 1985. Bewilderingly, one of the most inspirational of men on the pitch never achieved success in management. But he knew, really knew, what it was all about.

Stoic and always private about his own problems to the very end, Moore also mentioned Frank Senior who played for him when he managed Southend in the Fourth Division. Bobby Moore was there for his love of football and Frank Senior because of his love and respect for Moore.

And, of course, loyalty for where they both came from.

They had a relationship which resonates now in the career of Frank Lampard Junior. Frank is not coy about encouraging or praising his team-mates. Sure, he wants to score the goals – that's where the glory is – but the essential lesson he's learned is that you are nothing without the club. You have to earn your place and work to keep it. If you are on the bench, you might as well be in the Falkland Islands. Bobby Moore, for all the accolades, knew that, 'When youngsters join a club they copy the pros. If they are copying pros who arrive in the morning, sit down and read the paper and dash off as soon as training ends, that's how they are going to grow up.

'They should learn the good habits that were instilled in us at West Ham. Everybody wants players who are prepared to work that little bit extra.

'It's no coincidence that Frank [Lampard Senior] is still playing professional football at age thirty-seven. It's because he's strived to keep up a standard of fitness and a high level of performance. He would always do that little bit extra. What happens? Someone else follows his example. Then someone else, and so it snowballs...'

Chapter Two
Daddy's Boy

'Dad has been the biggest influence of my career. If I had
a bad game for the school team, I'd get stick off him.'

FRANK LAMPARD JUNIOR

Young Frank Lampard had no need to use football as a
path out of inner-city poverty or problems. His father's
financial diligence had taken care of that. Remember, with
the Lampards it's football and family and vice versa.

'Dad had to wait a long time to get a son. I have two
older sisters and, when I was born, I reckon he just threw
the ball at my feet and said, "That's a football – kick it."

'I had a lot of football knowledge pumped into me from
an early age, but the other side of the coin of having a
father with his record is that you tend to be very self-
critical.'

His father says he took to football 'like a duck to
water', but he'd seen other youngsters' careers collapse,
so he arranged for his son to have a private education.
At Brentwood School, Frank Junior applied himself as
much to the books as to sport; he did exceptionally well

at cricket and as a very young lad was playing on youth soccer teams.

He went from kicking a ball around the garden at age six to Sunday-morning games with kids two and sometimes four years older than himself. If he'd been a swimmer they'd have chucked him in at the deep end.

'Frank never came to me and said he wanted to be a professional, it was one of those situations that just developed over the years. As an ex-pro, the first thing you want is for a son to kick a ball. His enjoyment was so obvious. Give him a ball and he would carry on until he dropped.'

He went on to play for Heath Park at youth level and there the parents of the other players complained that he was only in the team because of his father, because of his name.

It is one thing to take all the sticks and stones going at professional level, but suffering the smugness and stupidity of the small-minded needs anger management. Frank does it his way: 'I still feel that I am proving these people wrong whenever I go on to the field.'

And there were always pressures, 'Dad doesn't often show his feelings. He manages to get his point over pretty well, though. He's my biggest fan and my biggest critic. He always will be. We've had countless rows and arguments, but afterwards I usually realise he's right.

'There were times at home when we'd row over football because I refused to see things his way. I'm one of those blokes who says what he feels; I don't see any point in holding back.

'I know some of the things I've said to him have hurt like hell and I think, Oh, my God, what have I said? But when I've gone off and cooled down a bit, I admit to myself he has been in the game too long to be wrong too many times.

'He's still a bit of a hardman, a difficult taskmaster who strives for perfection. That bit rubbed off on me. I want my game to be perfect and I always want that bit of steel my dad had in his playing days.

'Being hard doesn't come naturally, but I have learned how to be strong, both mentally and physically.

'The rest of the family, my sisters, my mum, have also been a support. It was always football, football at home and sometimes it would do your head in. I'd go and talk to mum just to get a release.'

You can understand. For the family it has been a football world for a long, long time. Other matters were kept private, known only to a tiny inner circle.

Pat Lampard has been the perfect matriarch, knowing the family, their secrets, their foibles, strengths and weaknesses. She has held it all together over the years. She has the perfect personality for it. She also has a pragmatic sense of humour about the family circle.

When Frank Junior was excelling at cricket at Brentwood School, there was much talk of him becoming a professional cricketer, even of representing his country. He was that good. There were moves by coaches from the South of England Independent Schools to enlist young Frank as a future cricket star. It led to a front-room talk between mum and dad.

'Any question of football or cricket?' Frank Senior was asked.

'The boy can do what he likes,' said his father who walked out the door. About thirty seconds ticked away.

Then the door opened and Frank Senior's head came around it and with a smile he added, 'He can do what he likes as long as he plays football...' The family business.

Harry Redknapp joined the Hammers, aged seventeen, as an apprentice in 1964. 'I lived in the East End. I was born ten minutes from the ground; Bobby, Geoff, Martin, Frank and Trevor Brooking, they all came from within twenty minutes of the ground.'

Frank Senior was eight years old when he first started kicking a ball at Upton Park and fifteen years old when he was being coached by the legendary Ron Greenwood ('the only one great coach', according to Harry Redknapp) at West Ham. Then, the insistence and thrust of training was on invention and speed of movement – the traditional qualities of the club.

His son signed his Youth Training Scheme papers with West Ham, ignoring the temptations of Arsenal and Spurs, on 1 August 1992, when he was close to the same age.

'I wasn't even working with West Ham when he decided to sign his YTS forms – he made the final decision to play for the Hammers,' said Frank Senior, adding, 'He was very lucky. A lot of my old mates from Canning Town still watch West Ham from the terraces. All of them were football nuts, just like me, desperate to play for the local side. I managed to get there.

'I felt I was representing them, those blokes who

wanted to be out there on the pitch busting a gut for their club.

'The same thing happened to Frank. A lot of his pals stood on the same terraces doing exactly the same as my mates. Frank realised he was their standard bearer – he wanted to give them his best, just as I wanted to give them mine.'

His son revealed, 'I nearly went to Spurs, but in the end I chose West Ham. It was the club I supported, after all.'

And there were family ties. Harry Redknapp moved from Bournemouth in 1992 to become assistant to manager Billy Bonds at West Ham. He's addicted to the game and team control, although he warns, 'In football management, you can leave home full of the joys of spring and come home in despair and, if you don't feel like that, you shouldn't be in it.'

His nephew found out quickly how much jealousy is around. Even then it was something of a curse to be Frank Lampard Junior, even though his father had left the club seven years earlier. And he was still small for his age and could not get around the pitch as much as he would have liked. That changed.

Frank Lampard Senior was a successful businessman with a thriving property business; the family home was a smart, large house in Romford, Essex, but even as a young teenaged trainee there were lads telling him he was only there because of his dad.

He's a proud man and was a proud boy: the criticism and sniping upset him, but he kept his rebellion against his tormentors within himself; he learned early to keep his most dramatic ups and downs and his thinking as private as possible. As would become the norm, he just worked harder to prove his right to be in the stimulating environment of the West Ham 'Academy'.

There had been some famous graduates, most memorably the 1966 World Cup trio of Bobby Moore, Geoff Hurst and Martin Peters of whom, for many, Frank Junior brings back many footballing memories.

With his great friend Rio Ferdinand and Trevor Sinclair, Frank Junior comprised, nearly four decades on, a superbly talented reminder of the glorious ghosts of the past. Of course, by then it could also have been called the Fame Academy.

Harry Redknapp has always made a great deal of 'his' boys nourished at West Ham United. In 1994, when he took over as manager from Billy Bonds, he brought back a former graduate – Frank Lampard Senior. The former club full-back had been working part-time with the club, scouting and coaching.

His property business was so successful that it cost him financially to return to full-time football as West Ham's assistant manager. 'I had a lot of things to consider, but the lure of the job proved too much. If it had been anyone else but Harry and any other club but West Ham I wouldn't have done it. When I did, I couldn't wait to get there every morning and get the tracksuit on.'

But, with two Frank Lampards at West Ham, the accusations of nepotism intensified.

Twentieth-century legendary player turned 21st-century newspaper columnist Jimmy Greaves, who began his playing career at Chelsea and ended it at West Ham, wrote about the family connections, to which Harry Redknapp responded, 'It was a hurtful article. It wasn't as if I was employing my brother-in-law from the local fish and chip shop. I couldn't have been luckier than getting Frank to agree to work with me.'

And, being the man he is, Frank Lampard Senior was going out of his way not to do his son any favours. The advice as always: 'Let your football do the talking.'

His father also explained some facts of footballing fame, 'I told him that all players have to suffer a bit of abuse at times, even the great Bobby Moore. It's how you deal with it that's important. I always found it a little ironic, because young Frank was representing the fans on the pitch. He was claret and blue right through.'

Yet, the envy-hampered doom watchers, those who always believe that the offspring of the famous or the rich or talented will always fall foul of a parent's shadow, stood back and waited, or offered anonymous jibes from the terraces.

Young Frank wasn't as thick-skinned then as he would become. He hadn't the experience. He was soon to get it. It made him grow up quickly. He was lucky. He'd got an excellent education. He'd also got a diploma from the school of hard knocks.

Chapter Three
School of Hard Knocks

'You try to ignore the criticism, but it can hurt. And it did.'

FRANK LAMPARD JUNIOR

When Pat Lampard used to shout 'Frank!', wanting to attract her son or husband around the house, the response of the two men was usually silence. She must want the other one. Pat says they both were convinced it was always the other Frank. Certainly, that is what they told her. 'I used to ignore her and pretend it was Dad she was after. He did the same,' said Frank Junior. It was the other shouting that got to him, though.

He was bright, he had dealt capably with his education and his future was clear to him: all he had to do was play football to the best of his ability, to learn, to improve and to go on. He had an extraordinary support system. Yet the fans were telling him to stuff it. And much, much worse besides.

When Frank Junior started with West Ham all he wanted was to be in the first team. In the middle of the night in his room at the family home in Romford, he would see himself as a star striker, as Roy of the Rovers. It was many a schoolboy's fantasy, but for Frank when the 7am alarm went off it could become a reality.

His cousin Jamie Redknapp was establishing himself as a formidable football player. He had to keep working, just as his father kept insisting. There were other things in life than football, but then...

'Part of the reason for the progress I have made is that I made a conscious effort when I was sixteen or seventeen that I needed to add more to my game. I could always hit the pass and be neat and tidy. But that extra bit, of scoring goals and being box to box, just gives more to your game. You realise you need that part to your game if you are going to be a complete player. I think it was probably Dad as well who drummed that into me.'

But many of the fans believed his progress, his elevation, was only because of his father. And once you pick up that particular stick it tends to grow branches.

When he made his first appearance as a substitute for West Ham in January 1996, a section of the Upton Park crowd started booing. It was hurtful and menacing and upset many of those present. What young lad needed this sort of treatment?

Certainly, the professionals saw how unpleasant and unnecessary it was; the much-liked, affable Scot Gordon Strachan, then the Coventry manager, who had brought himself on at the same time as Frank, put his arm round him to console him.

Frank was just seventeen years old and it has to rank as

one of the cruellest introductions any player has undergone. Yet, his father emphasised, probably more optimistically than realistically, 'He never let it worry him. He showed them what a terrific temperament he's got. He took it in his stride. They thought it was nepotism, but it wasn't. Harry and I knew what he could do. He was there on merit.'

Frank admitted, 'I was young when I started getting all the remarks. It is hard for someone that age to take it because you have no experience. You try to ignore the criticism, but that little bit can hurt you and it did. There were boos and comments and that was disappointing. The reception I got never made me think I should leave; I was always West Ham from the start.

'The fact was I had always been a West Ham fan and wanted to play for them, but there were comments. It might have been a good thing because it made me a stronger personality.

'When it started I'd only just broken into the team and I still had to prove myself to them. It wasn't easy at times and I took some stick from a few fans in the early games. I had to cope with it, but it was a big problem for me.

'People looking in from the outside might see it as an advantage having family connections, but the stick I got when I first broke through at West Ham was disappointing to say the least.

'I talk to people in everyday life who have dads who run their business and they realise how hard it has been for me. The only advantage was that it may have made me a stronger character. The frustration was not being able to prove yourself in an instant.

'Before I had a chance to really produce the goods in the first team, people were very sceptical, wondering if I was only there because of the family connections. All I ever got was the accusation that I was only playing because of my dad and my uncle. I needed mental toughness because of all the things that get said when your father has a senior position at the club.

'It would have been so easy for me to have buckled, to have run away and hidden when the stick was flying as I was struggling to get my game together.

'I'd hear the effing and blinding from the terraces. Both at home and away. "You're not as good as your old man." "You're not fit to lace his boots."

'It hurt. It piled on the pressure. I worked twice as hard to prove myself to the manager who picked the team – and to the fans. It's not any fun but it makes you stronger; you want to prove them so wrong. I suppose the advantage from a young age is that people recognise you and you stand out because of your name.

'And then there's the disadvantage… People call you a kid at twenty, but at seventeen years old I had pretty much just come out of school and I was getting booed by grown men.

'It's tough for any player who is a victim of the boo-boys. It knocks at your confidence and gets under your skin. I honestly don't think people realise what damage they can do to a player. But I know you have to be able to take it on the chin in this game and be big enough to take the flak and come back for more if necessary.'

Of course, there's no proving them wrong without the chances to play regularly. It was Catch-22. So, as ever, he got on with it, but it was frustrating as he warmed the substitutes' bench week after week waiting for a moment, just a moment, to prove himself in action.

And, ironically, the most vicious bile from the West Ham stands, the crescendo of booing and scathing charges that were almost impossible to accept, arose because of his desire to show the fans how much he deserved to be on the pitch. And the management's belief that he could do it. The fans thought they knew better. The charges were of graft, of a scam – that it was just a way to make money.

Frank Senior explained, 'A lot of it came about because Frank made a few appearances as a substitute in his first season, coming on in the last five minutes. A lot of the punters thought we were just trying to sort him out with appearance money bonuses. The reality was that the Lampards would have paid West Ham to let Frank Junior loose every moment of every game.

'The fact is that Frank's done it the hard way, all off his own back,' says his father, adding, 'He'd done it under his own steam. People forget how young he is.'

Or, more importantly, how young he was.

Nobody can contain the fans' fury, though. Nor their fun or their superior Variety Club inventiveness. They can spot a player's weakness before he's even aware of it.

Frank had to endure more scurrilous personal abuse. There were the 'Fat Frank' jibes about his wobbly backside and the nasty 'Poor Man's Jamie' (a mangle of nepotism with Harry and being a cousin of Jamie). Invective under the bridge you'd think for a veteran like Harry Redknapp, but he revealed of his management days with both Franks at West Ham. 'I couldn't sleep without a gulp of Night Nurse. Otherwise, even when things were going well, by one in the morning I'd be awake, my mind racing. It's very difficult to explain. I can't tell you how low I could get on a Saturday night. When things are bad it's like a death in the family.

'But the stress doesn't come from the board. Never, ever. Or the fans. And I didn't have problems with the players. It's within, knowing that so many people care about the football club that you run, you've got all those hopes on your shoulders.'

Harry Redknapp, an ongoing if sometimes long-distance influence, with his brother-in-law, on one of England's most important players, has a crafty Cockney image; it's easy word processing to make him part Del Trotter with a sprinkling of George Cole's wheeler-dealer in *Minder*. He's way ahead of that game.

Harry Redknapp has the wit and intelligence and, most necessarily, the assurance to win at football which is a far more complex, entertaining and intriguing act than ducking and diving. Young Frank Lampard benefited from that, as had his father, at West Ham. But he suffered from the connection too, as Redknapp recalled in his book, 'I was disappointed in sections of the West Ham crowd which gave him no end of stick during his early appearances. The crowd was getting at me for playing him and Frank Senior didn't think I was playing him enough! We never fell out over it, but I was aware Frank thought I was bringing his son along too slowly. I'd been through the same situation with Jamie and I was confident I was doing what was right.'

Chapter Four

The New Academy

'Being best mates with Rio Ferdinand helped my son.'

FRANK LAMPARD SENIOR

School was nearly over and young Frank was a supremely ambitious and dedicated member of the Upton Park Academy. In the mid-1990s, Harry Redknapp and Frank Lampard Senior were nourishing a group of young players; Frank Junior was starting to graduate from schoolboy player to contender. There was also Rio Ferdinand, who as a fourteen-year-old would go round to tea at the Lampards, and Trevor Sinclair and Joe Cole were waiting in the wings. It was all bubbling nicely and many said they had England's best youth team.

The players and the form sped on. Harry and Frank Senior's West Ham won the FA Youth Cup. Frank Junior, Rio and Joe Cole were seen as pivotal to English football's future. Joe Cole in those days was anointed as the player who would wear Gazza's crown, the most exciting prodigy since Paul Gascoigne first fizzed and whizzed huge bursts of energy into Newcastle.

Rio had advertised himself as an attacking midfielder. In the second leg of a Youth Cup final against Chelsea, playing just behind the main striker, he scored one, made two and, though only a schoolboy in a fully fledged youth team, announced his self-belief by successfully taking one of the penalties in the shoot-out.

'That was when I first realised he was top class,' recalled his friend Frank Junior adding, 'He was brilliant that night. From that moment, the question changed from "can he play?" to "where should he play?"'

Frank learned. He watched Rio make the game come to him rather than the other way round, which his father had always told him was one of Bobby Moore's great, almost perfect, skills.

Martin Peters is a great fan of his former club's graduates. He predicted Frank and Rio's breakthroughs before they happened, when they were still both teenagers, 'I look at the old videos and I'm thinking, Hey, Mooro, what are you doing up there? I'm amazed how far forward he got sometimes. The equalising goal in '66, Mooro was brought down by Overath well forward for the free-kick.

'I think Rio can do that once he's got the confidence. He's got the quickness of feet; he's just got to learn to pick and choose the moment and the passes. Bobby wasn't the quickest, but he was very rarely found out because he read the game better than anyone I ever knew, but that took time. Rio's not the finished article and, at nineteen, he shouldn't be thrown in the deep end too early. He has pace and he's got time on the ball, especially at home.'

Of course, at West Ham in the late 1990s, Harry

Redknapp reckoned he had the nucleus of a seriously good football side, with Rio, Joe Cole and Frank Lampard always talked up and compared to Moore, Hurst and Peters, the Class of '66.

Yet nostalgia doesn't pay much of a dividend. The point of football is to go forward, not back. That's where you find the glory. 'Appy 'Arry never produced his crystal ball, but he still predicted that the rest of the magic spell could be cast around that particular talented trio. It was all interesting, but, as with many things in football, just a theory.

What Frank Lampard Junior wanted was action. He got his first full chance of it in August 1996, at the beginning of the season. Then all the talk post-Euro '96 was about foreign players: spending in the Premier League had swelled to a loudly talked-about and unprecedented £90 million. Nearly a decade later it looks like small change. Then, it emphasised that foreign was best. Or certainly thought to be so.

Harry Redknapp's West Ham, known as 'The United Nations', got a different look with the introduction of old-fashioned East End local boy Frank Lampard for the 17 August 1996 match against Arsenal (which the Gunners won 2–0).

Redknapp admitted at the time, 'Over the last couple of seasons I have been as responsible as anyone for going abroad to buy players. For me the reason was simple. We couldn't afford the prices being asked at home for the quality needed. But nothing gives me greater pleasure than seeing one of our lads come up through the ranks and it could be a dream for me if in a few years we could field a team full of locals.

'The trouble has been that the club which used to pride itself on producing its own players had a barren patch. Last season we saw Danny Williamson make an impact and now young Frank has got his chance. I feel that this will be the first of many, many games at the club for him.

'He is an outstanding prospect who can go a long way. The same goes for Rio Ferdinand who would have played had Slaven Bilic not declared himself fit. Frank and Rio are the first of a very healthy crop.'

Yet, it was Frank who had spent much of the 1996–97 season on the substitutes' bench while Rio Ferdinand earned the plaudits. Frank says Rio's swift advancement inspired him and maybe it did, but surely masochistically. 'The fact that Rio got so much praise helped me, too. Rio and I went about everywhere together and I didn't begrudge him a thing. When Rio broke in he got loads of accolades and it was all totally deserved. Maybe that was the little jolt I needed. I saw Rio getting all the praise and getting in the side and I thought, I want that. And I went for it. I pulled my finger out and I came back determined to get my own thing going.'

His father said, 'Being best mates with Rio helped my son. Ron Greenwood used to talk about professional jealousy and that can be a good thing. Rio reached the height quicker than Frank, but it spurred Frank on. He saw what happened to Rio and he wanted some of it.'

There was family strife as he played passionately to get his own headlines. Frank Junior was struggling to get into the first team. His father had total professional, as opposed to parental, belief in his son. He was pushing for his boy. Harry Redknapp? He had a difficult hand to play. But he knew how strong his hand was and, back in 1996, talked about the two Franks with commendable, utter confidence in his instincts and knowledge. 'Young Frank is a completely different sort of player. He is a central midfielder and right-footed, whereas his father was a left-footed full-back.

'I think he is going to be a really good player. He doesn't give the ball away and has the knack of scoring goals. I don't expect him to be pushing regularly in the first team until next year, but he has won his chance.

'Frank certainly hasn't been shown any favouritism. The senior professionals know if a bloke is good enough and if he wasn't he would soon be shot down. But senior pros aren't stupid, they pick who can play a bit and this boy can play. They know he is good. He is six foot, mobile, has a soccer brain and scores goals. He is an exceptional talent. Frank wants to be a player and he will be. I've complete faith in him. There's no favouritism here. I picked Frank because he's good. It's as simple as that. I had a similar situation with my son Jamie at Bournemouth. He will be a first-team regular by the start of next season.'

Years on, he said, 'Frank Lampard my brother-in-law I will love forever. I love the man. Were Frank and Frank being persecuted for being father and son? Not by me. But maybe by circumstances.'

Frank Junior rose above them. In West Ham's 1997–98 season, he endorsed the faith he had in himself, which was more than enough to convince most other people. He just wanted his chances, like the opening game of the season on 9 August 1997, the hottest day of the year. Frank sizzled, too, against Barnsley.

West Ham had won just once on the opening day of the season in their past ten attempts. It didn't look any better. As the second half began they were trailing by one goal. Then John Hartson nodded in an equaliser for the Hammers. Frank then scored West Ham's winner with a quarter of an hour remaining.

He flicked the ball past David Watson thirty seconds after having come on as a substitute. Headline? Phew, what a scorcher! He kept driving forward, but there was no sudden leap to first-team fame. It's been that way with him: first Rio got the glances and attention and later, in Euro 2004, Wayne Rooney, as Frank moved his game and career up a gear.

He has always been in the business of building dreams, putting down foundations for that climb to the very top. But there were distractions. There were also temptations. And he was only a teenager.

Chapter Five

La Dolce Vita

'He's a great friend, man and footballer.'
RIO FERDINAND ON FRANK LAMPARD, OCTOBER 2004

Footballers were more sought after than rock stars, and Frank and the other lads from the Academy were millionaires in the making, magnets for all the glamour and glitter that goes with the money.

Frank and Rio – 'best pals since they had their backsides hanging out of their trousers', according to Harry Redknapp – got England glory at the same time. At different levels. Now, they were beginning to get splendid – no backsides showing – in their Prada and Versace suits, parading in their Gucci and Ferragamo shoes. Richard James made their shirts, Hermes their trays of ties. Tiffany wasn't just in *EastEnders* any more; it was where you bought your cufflinks.

Frank made his debut in the England Under-21 team against Greece in Crete on 13 November 1997. Tall (6ft 3in) Rio, five months his junior (born in London's Peckham on 7

November 1978), made his first full England appearance in a friendly against Cameroon at Wembley the same month.

In the previous weeks they had both run into trouble with drinking and the bosses of their England squads. Frank and Rio were both early starters with West Ham.

South-East Londoner Rio began his schoolboy football years playing as a centre-forward. He later moved to central midfield and it was at Eltham Town Under-14s that he attracted the West Ham scouts. At fourteen, he was signed as a schoolboy and two years later stayed on, despite attracting interest from both Middlesbrough and Chelsea.

On a two-year YTS contract (on £30 a week) as an apprentice, he and Frank helped the club's youth team to win the South-East Counties League with a record number of points. Harry Redknapp signed him on his first professional contract when he turned seventeen years old.

Harry Redknapp had sent Frank off to Swansea on loan in October 1995, and a year later he followed on the 'character-building' method by dispatching Rio to Bournemouth for eight weeks from November 1996. It paid dividends for the two lads: if Frank was the new Martin Peters, then Rio's performances urged comparisons with Bobby Moore.

They were both earning fantastic wages for their ages, and their lifestyles, the designer clothes, the cool cars, reflected their wealth.

Glenn Hoddle was England manager and he called up Rio for a World Cup qualifier against Moldova in 1997. Rio went out to celebrate. After an evening drinking with friends, he was stopped as he was driving home and the result was a twelve-month driving ban. He also missed the World Cup game, dropped from the senior squad. 'I understood why Glenn Hoddle had no alternative but to leave me out of the team. At the time I was worried that Glenn would never pick me again.'

What he said next reminds us that these big, strong lads are just that – lads: 'But I think I was more scared about telling my mum. It took me a whole day to pluck up the courage to break the news to her. In the end she was really understanding and helped me sort everything out with the police. I knew I had made a stupid mistake and I learned from it.'

Rio said that after the drink-driving conviction he still used to drink, but that he was careful before matches. He liked going to nightclubs and bars and added, 'I hang out a lot with Frank Lampard. A lot of the West Ham players are married with kids, so they don't tend to come out as much. Frank and I go out.'

Women? As teenagers, their pin-ups were model Helena Christensen, Denise Van Outen and two of the 1990s stars of *EastEnders*, Martine McCutcheon and Michelle Collins, Tiffany and Cindy.

Rio had set up Frank with Mariama Goodman, the full-figured singer with Sweet Honeyz, but he said, 'We're not bothered about having proper girlfriends, all the hassle that goes with commitment and relationships. I take girls out on dates sometimes, but I worry if they are going to go off and sell their stories to newspapers if we split up. I think it's harder to trust people once you're famous.'

Both he and his best friend would find that out. They had already learned that there are consequences – for everything.

The month before their different England debuts, they ran into trouble in Italy. Part of the Under-21 squad, the two of them, along with Wimbledon's Ben Thatcher and Liverpool pair Danny Murphy and Jamie Carragher, were caught in a bar in the Italian town of Rieti. It was the afternoon of the senior side's World Cup clash against Italy in Rome.

The Under-21 players had beaten Italy 1–0 the previous day and were allowed to go shopping on the day of the World Cup match, provided they returned in time to check out of their hotel ready for the trip to Rome. Under-21 coach Peter Taylor got a telephone call from a local bar owner complaining that some English players were becoming rowdy.

He was angry his players had not returned to the hotel and were drinking in a bar just a few hours before England's big game. All five were sent home immediately by a furious Taylor and missed seeing the big game. Taylor recalled that he had no alternative but to punish the five: 'I'm here to help the players. They probably didn't think that at the time, but it was a lesson well learned.

'The players knew I was disappointed. They rang me at home and apologised. They just stepped out of line and it is something I had to show a bit of strength on.'

Taylor, who would become a good friend to and supporter of Frank Lampard's first-squad hopes, had told the West Ham manager of the players involved and Harry

Redknapp left the discipline to him. 'I was happy to let him deal with it. It was a painful lesson to both players.'

But not too painful. Frank and Rio were included in the squad for the first leg of the European Championship play-off against Greece in Crete on 13 November. Rio went up a squad, but for Frank it was a start on the national ladder; soon he would be captain of the Under-21 team.

And around the same time footballing life was looking grand at Upton Park. It's hard to pick a breakthrough moment, but the Coca-Cola Cup, when West Ham took down Walsall 4–2 on 19 November 1997, was when Frank clearly took on the responsibility to score goals as well as to make them. He knows that when he gets a goal his total game is tuned to perfection: it's proof that he's playing at his highest level.

In the Walsall game he scored in fifteen minutes and in the second half produced two more winners within moments. His hat-trick made headlines. Matt Dickinson reported in *The Times* on 27 November 1997: 'West Ham United can still claim to be an academy, their latest young talent, Frank Lampard, displaying his burgeoning talents last night with an impressive hat-trick that spared his team from some anxious moments in a treacherous Coca-Cola Cup fourth-round tie.

'The midfield player made his England Under-21 debut in Crete last week shortly before his team-mate, Rio Ferdinand, arrived in the senior team with such aplomb. Both kept their calm against lively Nationwide League Second Division opponents, when more senior colleagues were looking decidedly ragged.

'With Walsall threatening to come back from two goals behind, Lampard steered West Ham into the quarter-finals with two second-half goals in sixty seconds to add to his opening strike after fifteen minutes. Harry Redknapp, his manager, believes he has more to add to his impressive passing skills as he matures.'

'I get immense pleasure that we are starting to get some kids coming through,' Redknapp said. 'It's been almost ten years since we produced players of any real note and now I have Frank and Rio coming through and there are more behind them.

'I am especially pleased for Frank because, let's be honest, when he first got in the side he did not get a very good reception, which we were all disappointed about. People maybe thought something stupid like he was getting his chance because his old man is here, but I always knew he would be a good player and now he is getting stronger.'

Other newspaper reports on 20 November 1997 also gave a good insight into the changing media and public perception of the teenaged Frank. This is an edited, composite version: 'Frank Lampard celebrated the first hat-trick of his blossoming career as West Ham reached the Coca-Cola Cup quarter-finals with a hard-earned win against Second Division Walsall.

'Everyone at Upton Park thinks Lampard has a great future in the game, despite the way the crowd were slow to respond to him when he first came into the side.

'But it was West Ham's physical presence and strength in the tackle as much as Lampard's goals that put them into the last eight of the competition for the first time in seven years.

'Foreign influence is not just changing the game in the Premiership. It stretches down to the Second Division and there is probably more good football being played at all levels in this country than in any other era. Walsall were gunned down in two quickfire bursts of goal scoring. The brilliant Israeli Eyal Berkovic laid on simple chances for Lampard in the eighteenth minute and for the Premiership's leading scorer, John Hartson, sixty seconds later. It was Hartson's sixth of the season in the competition and his fourteenth in all. Walsall dictated most of the play until well into the second half. But then Lampard, whose finishing has improved enormously in recent weeks, scored two more in as many minutes. Lampard got the official award, but hat-trick men usually do.'

For Frank, it was the beginning of his seduction of the Upton Park sceptics, although he revealed, 'Dad didn't even say much then. But I could tell by the look on his face that he was pleased with me. I've always tried to follow Dad's example, the way he conducts himself at the club and away from it. I hope I made him proud. It wasn't easy with my dad at the club and there was a time when I thought it might be better if I went somewhere else, but I got over that.

'With the fans I felt that I was winning them over with each performance. But you were on audition all the time. It was pressure. It drove me on.'

Chapter Six

Goodbye Junior

'Nobody can say he doesn't deserve his chance.'

HARRY REDKNAPP ON FRANK LAMPARD'S FIRST
ENGLAND CALL UP IN APRIL 1999

Frank Lampard was like a young stallion – he just could not wait to be set free. He kept working. He kept improving. He kept waiting to be noticed. He was playing game after game for the England Under-21 team and was now its captain. He had proved himself to almost everybody; now when he touched the ball there were cheers, not jeers, from the West Ham fans.

Yet, it was only in 1998 that the official West Ham programme reflected the wishes of their superstar-in-waiting. Frank Lampard the player would be listed without any other identification. From then on, to distinguish the two, his father would be called 'Senior' rather than him 'Junior'. Frank believed he had lost that tag months and months earlier, and he had, but for him it was like getting the key to the front door. And the family car. He was trusted out on his own.

'I realised I had to get rid of that tag, otherwise it was going to plague my career at West Ham. It always upset me as a teenager. I always wanted to do my best and I worked hard at it, but there were such big sections of people out there not willing to give me a fair chance. I suppose I did feel persecuted. Maybe since I lost the Junior bit it's been easier for me to get on and play my own game.

'It's very clear cut when you're younger. You don't always understand the full picture. And it is a very self-absorbing life.'

And that is something that stars, in whatever game, are always slow to take in, to fully understand. Frank, though, always has seen the positive, if sometimes painful, aspects of his legacy. 'In terms of character building, being known as Frank Lampard Junior made me more of my own man. Having that tag made me stronger; I had a lot to prove and to live up to. When I became the focus and I lost the Junior tag, it was easier to get on and play my own game without any problems.'

Fans forget how long he suffered abuse from the terraces – from his own club's followers. The Hammers fans only truly began to accept him towards the end of 1997 after fifteen starts for the first team and seventeen appearances as a substitute. And he still had to keep proving himself. As fickle as fame is, they were now talking of him being another Martin Peters.

But Lampard, the stallion, had to keep marking his time, and desperately trying not to show his frustration in public. He felt as though he was on the West Ham substitutes' bench again. When would it happen for him?

Presumably, Glenn Hoddle, himself a magnet for ill will, could identify with Frank's victimisation, reviled and lambasted, and the butt of the boo-boys' bile. And Hoddle had promised 'youth' a chance for England's friendly against the Czech Republic on 18 November 1998. So, playing against Chelsea ten days earlier felt very much like a first-team audition, almost a dress rehearsal. Hoddle was also aware of what a firm favourite Frank was at West Ham.

That was emphasised when many of the West Ham faithful turned out to watch him captain the Under-21s in east London against Bulgaria. He had received a huge reception – and scored the winner; the highlight of his England Under-21 career. He'd watched Michael Owen and friends like Rio and Kieron Dyer graduate from the Under-21s.

The chance of grown-up international glory was around the corner for Frank. Or so it seemed. But not this time. He was severely disappointed having performed so well for the Under-21s in the previous two matches, but he did not sulk. He vowed to get his head down and work even harder – the Lampard family answer to all hurdles.

Indeed, as always, the rejection appeared to fire Frank on. Which is why his call-up to the England team in April 1999 was all the more gratifying for him. He'd had his disappointments in World Cup year 1998; he'd made the 'B' team for a warm-up game against Chile, but that wasn't the real thing.

When the fax arrived at Upton Park telling him that Kevin Keegan had picked him for the squad to face Hungary in Budapest it was a moment of celebration. But there were the old doubts. His dad had been in the Under-23 squad with Keegan. Would there be criticism? Then he told himself, 'My dad doesn't pick the England team.'

When Hoddle had been ignoring him, Peter Taylor had kept his spirits up. Taylor would call Frank and tell him to stick at his game, that his time would come. 'He was always there for me when I was disappointed at not making the senior squad. When I did he was the first to ring and congratulate me.'

When Frank flew off to Budapest, Harry Redknapp took pleasure in saying, 'When I first saw Frank as a kid I knew he could become a player, but now he's got belief in himself as well. I remember when we gave him and Rio their debuts. I said then they could go all the way and nobody can say he doesn't deserve his chance.'

But he didn't get it. He made it as far as the bench. Commentators wondered if he was held back because of his importance to the Under-21s. At that time Frank refused to go near that argument and still does. He'd been part of the young England team which beat Poland 5–0, regarded as the best performance ever by an Under-21 side. He'd been an inspirational captain.

But Frank *was* wanted by West Ham's rivals. Spurs and Aston Villa were both keen to sign him; he was rated at around £7 million. Early in 1999, Spurs punted a £4 million bid and after that was rejected were increasing the money.

Harry Redknapp was furious about attempts to kidnap 'his' boys. At the time he fumed, 'We're not looking to sell our young players. Why should we? It annoys me when I hear Tottenham are going to sign Frank Lampard. Why should he go to Spurs? Why shouldn't we think big. We're not second-class citizens. If we sell the Frank Lampards, Rio Ferdinands and the Joe Coles of this world, we will never be up there with the big boys.'

Harry Redknapp? Crystal ball? There was no need for second sight for that analysis. Time would tell the story. Frank was still with West Ham when the England dream finally did become reality. By then he'd played fourteen games for the Under-21s and scored seven goals. His goal ratio was as good as any front-line striker and he said, 'The team had been together for eighteen months and that helped a lot. I see scoring as a big part of my game and I work on it in training all the time. It's also about showing entertainment.'

Kevin Keegan brought him into the squad to play Belgium (England won 2–1 at Sunderland) on 10 October 1999. It was wonderful timing, as it helped his father and uncle rebut some bizarre claims by his former team-mate Eyal Berkovic, who had left West Ham for Celtic early in the year in a £5.5 million transfer deal.

In his book, written in Hebrew, the player accused Frank Lampard Senior of being racist. He said in his book, 'I can straightforwardly and without hesitation say that Lampard Senior absolutely hates foreigners. He would always sit down with British players and you would find him talking about us foreign players.'

In the book the Israeli player said Frank Senior ignored him and was not interested in the progress of other players – all he cared about was his son. He accused him of having 'unhealthy control' over Harry Redknapp.

He claimed that the manager and his assistant had no control over their players who stayed out until the early hours of the morning. Berkovic reserved most of his venom for Frank Senior: 'He would never join the foreign side when we played England against the foreigners in training. I would see him sitting with the home players talking about us.

'The fact remains this is not a place for foreign players to come to and I only managed so well because I have such a strong will.'

He seemed to have one prime target and shouted in print, 'The source of all the problems was Frank Lampard the father, the man who did everything to build the image of his son above every other player. I don't doubt Frank Lampard Junior is a good player, he may be an excellent player, but he is not a superstar and that's what his father tried to make him. Everything he did was aimed at making him the club superstar.

'I believe Frank Lampard used his family connections to take advantage of situations at the club. I was moved to the bench for a month despite the fact that I was playing well. I could see who was pulling the strings and began to understand the dynamics of the relationship between Harry Redknapp and Frank Lampard Senior. At one stage I was dropped because Frank Senior wanted Frank Junior to play up front.

'Whenever I played, Frank was a better player – my assists gave him 90 per cent of his goals. Young Frank knew when he had a good player alongside him, but his father wasn't interested in all of that – he just wanted the stage left open for his son.

'I remember during one game when I was on the bench I actually saw and heard Harry ask Frank when he was going to get me into the game. All that happened was that Frank Lampard just shook his head in a very negative way. He was frightened I would take the success from his son.'

With his son in the England team – on merit – Frank Senior replied to the attack in a calm manner – as calm as the circumstances allowed: 'He must be paranoid or something. I have no problem at all with the foreign lads. If I did it would be a big problem, because the backbone of the squad is made up of foreign players.

'I work with them all and I even help those who come to me asking to do extra work after training. But I don't recall Eyal Berkovic asking to do extra work when he was here. Everything the lad is saying is simple nonsense and people will realise that once they stop and look at the real facts of what goes on at West Ham.

'The last thing you can accuse me or West Ham of is racism. As for the accusations of favouritism towards Frank, that's not true either. I'm only human, but in many ways I have made it harder for him.'

Such hard times were paying off for his son. What Frank had wanted most of all was a chance to prove himself not just for West Ham but for England. Now he was getting the chance. All the scouts knew he was a quick learner, a potential winner, and that potent mix of a midfielder who could get forward and score goals. It was elementary but beneficent alchemy, raising base material to stellar heights. A star is made, not born.

'Frank was always a potential World Cup-winning player

for England,' said a seasoned television pundit reflecting in 2005 on the breakthrough days. He added, 'He'll be captain in 2006 – he's got that sort of solid quality and background.

'If there's a chance of getting back the World Cup in 2006 – and wouldn't that be magical? – you have to believe in football and voodoo and every other sort of religion.

'And if there's any chance at all then Frank will be there... he's the leader of a gang that might just do it. The East End boys did it before. And they're not afraid of anything. Even voodoo. They might have invented that...'

Chapter Seven

Senior Service

'I want to win things.'
FRANK LAMPARD, SEPTEMBER 2000

Frank was winning hearts. He was a pin-up. The young lads of West Ham were making a name for themselves around town. There were parties and late nights, but not to their game's detriment. They were young enough. And fit enough. Especially for their growing army of female fans. Frank and Rio were quite a duo on the dating circuit.

Fashion-mad Rio had turned himself into a clotheshorse. Frank had moved from the family home to a sumptuous bachelor apartment in London's Knightsbridge. It was the superstar life for themselves and their footballing friends, earning tens of thousands of pounds a week. They were the business.

It was like joining a testosterone Derby. It was a Ferrari lifestyle with fabulous amounts of money spent on clothes, watches and cars – on having a good time. Frank had his East End wits about him, but it was a hell of a way

55

to live. Everything seemed on offer, from the glamour and the glitter to the girls.

For some reason he'd been attracted to singer Mariama Goodman who has publicly complained about having a 32-FF bust – 'tits to die for', according to one newspaper. So Jordan would have been of interest. We presume Frank spotted the cleavage before the smile. The larger-than-life supermodel revealed she thought Frank was a player in her world as well as on the pitch: 'Who knows how things might have turned out if I had met Frank Lampard at a different time in my life?

'As it was, there was never going to be anything other than a casual flirtation – the circumstances were all wrong. I met him out clubbing and, to be honest, I think he was almost as wild as me. We drank and flirted the night away. I ended up going back to his house with a group of friends. I stayed and he really tried it on with me. I fancied him a lot. Well, he's a good-looking bloke, isn't he?

'But kissing was as far as it went. When he was drunk he was one of the lads. Sober, he was a different bloke. I would have enjoyed getting to know him. But we never got together during the day. We met up clubbing a few times but that was that. He was convinced we could get together, but it was a bit too late – I couldn't help feeling regret.'

Frank was now part of a world of which television and series like *Footballers' Wives* only nick the surface. One of the circuit said, 'I know of one player who spent £26,000 a month on clothes, watches and jewellery. And another that has seventeen wardrobes stuffed with unworn designer clothes. Despite their high income, these players can end up thousands of pounds overdrawn at the end of the month. I know it doesn't seem possible.

'They take their cue from people such as David Beckham. But they don't earn David's money. Frank's the real thing – he will earn that sort of money one day and without having to marry a pop star. He and Rio used to joke that they weren't going to be Spice boys. And when he gets the money, you know it's not going to go in bling. Frank's from the land of diamond geezers – he's not the platinum jewellery sort. You can bet it will go in property like his dad. I think Frank's old man has sold more flats than he's kicked footballs. When his mobile goes, it's usually another punter wanting to buy. They're clever boys.'

And Gabby Yorath would not have been interested if Frank was not a serious person. She was hosting ITV's *On The Ball* when she met Frank. It was the roundabout world of football. Rio was dating Kirsty Gallagher and she introduced his friend to her friend. Frank and Gabby were soon seeing much of each other, especially in Richmond, Surrey.

Gabby, daughter of former Welsh football star Terry, was a footballers'/fans' fantasy. The beautiful game's number-one television sex symbol. And who did she fancy? She'd tried to avoid the footballers' trap, but Frank lured her in. According to one television pundit, she saw Frank as level headed and was attracted to him. He was very much smitten. The romantic potion worked, for a time.

At the same time as Frank became a more and more integral part of the West Ham team there was an increased need for magic of any variety at Upton Park. They'd finished in the top half of the Premiership for a couple of years, but it was a struggle. What makes a good club? Good management. What makes good management? Good players.

The magic, always the magic, is knowing how to play them – and handle them. But in the financial world of football – and Frank was to find himself in the luxury end – it's all about trade off and compromise. It's like Monopoly – the player with the most money should win. But who's running the Monopoly board?

With Rio, Frank and Joe Cole, Michael Carrick and Trevor Sinclair, Harry Redknapp had a multi-million-pound fund of assets. But club chairman Terry Brown had the key to the safe. In the summer of 1999, Frank had resisted attempts by Brown to contract him to West Ham for the foreseeable future.

There were lots of rumours – mainly surrounding Rio's future. But the word was West Ham would never sell Rio. That might have been because Harry Redknapp set the price too high. Whatever the reason, it was what Frank wanted to believe – and to hear. Fiercely ambitious, he knew he needed a winning club to prosper.

When Rio did sign and committed himself to West Ham in July 1999, his best friend did the same within forty-eight hours. Frank signed a £1-million-a-year deal set to run until 2005.

Frank had seen Rio, Paolo Di Canio and Ian Wright do better in the pay stakes; he was happier feeling he was getting something close to the money he was worth. The fans who had given him such a hard time had been lobbying for him to be given everything he wanted to stay with the club. When he did, he vowed to himself to help West Ham up the Premiership ladder and to get himself a permanent spot in the England senior squad. Still the undisputed Under-21 captain, his shot against Belgium appeared very much a one-off.

Yet, he played match after match, honing and improving his skills, and learning more and more that what others did was just as important as your own play; it's a team game. But West Ham were not having the best of times; yes, there were injuries, but something wasn't working for them. Frank was producing the driving football his team needed, but the goals were not multiplying as they should have done in their troubled season. Behind the scenes other figures were. Terry Brown wanted to sell Rio to Leeds for £15 million. He told his manager, 'Look, Harry, the transfer system's falling apart, we'll never get this offer again.'

Harry Redknapp tried to talk Brown out of it. He told Brown, 'Listen, they'll come back for more.'

Pause. Just a moment.

And Harry offered, 'And if not, Barcelona will buy him.'

Silence.

And Harry added, 'For he's the best.'

The chairman could not fathom that scenario. He argued, 'I can't see that.'

Three weeks after that conversation at Upton Park, Leeds United manager David O'Leary made another offer for Rio. A bid of £18 million. Redknapp had earned West Ham £1 million a week between the first and second offer. If you look at it Harry's way.

Terry Brown told him, 'Harry, we've got to take it.'

Harry replied, 'Yeah, I see that.'

And, you can certainly argue, that was the beginning of the end of Harry Redknapp and his brother-in-law and nephew at the Boleyn ground. Harry knew the game. Terry Brown knew the maths. Young Frank saw it all as a plot. He'd been told Rio would stay – and that's why he had hung on at West Ham. Now – now, this!

Seen from Rio's point of view, it was quite a leap forward, a rather large improvement, a multiple winner for a player who'd been seriously happy not too long before to get £30 a week. The world-record £18 million deal, a five-and-a-half-year contract worth £30,000 a week, made him the world's most expensive defender.

And Frank's dad had told him that scoring goals was where the business was? It was a time of mind games. For Rio it was an offer he could not refuse. O'Leary bemused the football world by breaking the British transfer record to buy Rio on 26 November 2000, with an astonishing fee for such a young defender.

Frank was confused. He just wanted his friend to stay a West Ham player. Rio was a hand to hold. But now he was playing a big boys' game. He complained that he had signed his deal under false pretences. Rough words were exchanged, but at the time he left it to his agent Steve Kuttner to offer them, 'When we signed that deal we were promised West Ham would never sell any of their top players. Frank is deeply upset and feels he has been double-crossed by the club.'

Later, a calmer Frank said, 'I was told Rio wouldn't be

sold and I was very upset when he was. I was surprised Rio went – and disappointed. I wish him well, and good luck to him, but I hope it doesn't send out the message that West Ham are only a selling club. That worries me.'

Harry Redknapp was in the middle, 'Frank was fed up about it, but we all showed the mental toughness needed to come to terms with the situation of Rio leaving. I was sorry to see him go, yet in a way I had a feeling of satisfaction that he made it. I have rucked him up hill and down dale in an effort to make him the player he is, and he has never answered me back. Personally, I don't think it's the hardest decision he'll ever have to make. And let's face it – how could we turn down £18 million?'

But Frank was not convinced. The seeds of discontent with West Ham were sown that winter. Within six months he got a telephone call from his mother Pat – and the West Ham Story was over. Or just about.

Chapter Eight

Sex, Sangria and Videotape

'I discovered among a hard core of Premiership footballers drug-taking is prevalent, group sex is the norm and you can buy your way out of almost anything.'

TELEVISION DIRECTOR BRUCE GOODISON, AUGUST 2004

Frank missed out on Euro 2000, but he made headlines anyway. For all the wrong reasons. He was filmed on video as he and other players had sex with a group of girls. He was on holiday in Ayia Napa in Cyprus that summer, as were Rio Ferdinand, Kieron Dyer and other household-name footballers. Also there was 'Tony', the man who filmed the footballers and their wild antics. The now infamous video was screened on national television in August 2004. It was used as part of the introduction to Bruce Goodison's 'faction' documentary *Sex, Footballers and Videotape*.

Goodison's film was commissioned by Channel 4 following the 'roasting' case in September 2003, in which a seventeen-year-old girl claimed she'd been raped by a group of men, including two Premiership players, at The Grosvenor House Hotel, London – both players were discharged without trial because the evidence against them was unreliable.

He dramatised several real-life incidents to form the narrative of his story, but explained, 'Before I started shooting the film I wanted to find out the truth – whether such incidents were the depraved indulgence of a few or indicative of a whole culture. I spoke to current and former players, their managers, security staff, agents and girls.

'Although they were happy to talk to me in the most graphic detail about their debauchery, and saw nothing wrong with their behaviour, none would be identified – for fear of the effect on their careers and reputations.

'I discovered among a hard core of Premiership footballers that drug-taking is prevalent, group sex is the norm and you can buy your way out of almost anything. There is, I was told, a little black book of available girls – and Premiership players know that, whatever town they are in, they are guaranteed an orgy or a gang bang if they contact these women.

'One of the seedier aspects of this brutally cynical attitude to sex is the way some footballers regularly film their exploits and pass videos and photographs among their friends.

'In my film, our characters use the cameras in their mobile phones to capture their exploits and send the images to their friends. This is not a fiction: this is regarded as perfectly normal behaviour among a clique of young footballers I talked to.'

The screening of Goodison's film brought back unwelcome memories for Frank. He, Rio and Kieron Dyer had been shamed by the *News of the World* in June 2000, after the newspaper obtained a copy of the video. Copies of the thirty-minute video, taken at the Grecian Bay resort at Ayia Napa, are now in circulation. It starts at a beach bar. In the first scenes, the camera focuses in on the breasts of one girl as she sits at a table. The cameraman says into the microphone, 'Come on, baby, come on, babe. I know you've got it in your game.'

The newspaper quoted one holidaymaker: 'They were drinking themselves into oblivion most days. They treated the women who flocked around them like pieces of meat.'

Yet, the girls were, it seems, delighted to be picked up by the famous football stars, and, seemingly, to have consensual sex with them. In all sorts of different ways. What the girls were indulging in never appears to be a trouble to them; it's only the filming that upsets them.

The reports of the antics were, of course, sensational in themselves, but, strangely, for such material, they were not overly prurient. Reading the stories which followed, it does appear that the England stars were given a fair deal of understanding.

It's the video itself which is so condemning. And the man who shot the film remains a matter of much controversy. When I approached him, in October 2004, I was told that he was 'too frightened to talk to you'. Frightened of whom?

'Leave it alone' was the message. And it continued to be so, despite formal, but not financial, offers for a conversation. Indeed, what more could be said? It was all already in the public domain.

On the video, girls go back to the players' rooms. The amateur moviemaker says on the tape, 'We are about to encrypt. If you really want to see the following programme you will have to pay £12.99.'

Yet the girls don't understand they are being filmed in all sorts of compromising situations. There appears to be a camera concealed close to Rio's bed. A naked, blonde-haired girl lies on his bed. Rio waves at the camera. He raises his hand over her head when she turns away, jerks a finger in her direction and laughs.

Then it features Kieron Dyer asleep with a girl. As the cameraman approaches the bed, they both wake up. The football star is not perturbed, but the girl shouts and pleads for the cameraman to go away. The cameraman laughs and says, 'Mr Dyer, King of Newcastle and Ipswich! You're the Don!'

On video Rio Ferdinand says he could keep going for another twenty-four hours: 'I'm out of my nut, but I know I could get through the whole day again. The way I'm feeling at the moment I could be in the swimming pool.'

Frank appears next with two girls who don't know they are being filmed. The video camera films a girl sitting on the bed performing a sex act on a naked Frank. Another man is having sex with another girl on the bed. The girl with Frank sees the camera and shouts, 'He's filming it!' Frank laughs. The other girl screams to the cameraman, 'Tony, get away!'

The *News of the World* reported the next scene for millions of people to read: 'Minutes later the footballer has clearly persuaded the girls that there will be no more degradation. Just then the cameraman returns and catches the blonde again performing a sex act on Lampard. He jeers as she whimpers: "No, oh no!" "Go on, look at the camera," Lampard orders. "I want you to look at it. Tell them you love it." "Tony, no filming!" she yells and tries unsuccessfully to push the camera away.

'By now her degradation is total and Lampard orders her to have lesbian sex with her friend on the bed. "**** her!" he grunts. Her friend replies: "No, I don't do that." But eventually the camera films them rolling naked and kissing on the bed. Next to them stands Lampard, looking down as he slurps from a bottle of Budweiser and splutters: "Go on, do it, darling. Go for it."

'Then the other man suggests an act so deviant with one of the girls that, even in her vulnerable state on the bed, she refuses.

'All the time Lampard is laughing wildly and spanking the blonde's backside. With each smack he exclaims: "Oooh – how's that!" Later, Lampard appears to try to convince the girls that they were not being filmed at all. He tells the spanked blonde: "He's not filming. He's just practising for when he comes to film."'

The next scene brings an encore from Kieron Dyer. He is filmed through a hotel window as he makes love to an unsuspecting girl from Manchester. But, as Dyer looks up at the camera, the girl turns around too and the cameraman runs from the balcony.

The video moves on to a hotel room with the same girl and two of Dyer's male friends. The disorientated girl sits on a bed as the three men discuss a 'foursome'. She is not interested. The newspaper reported: 'She can see the camera running, but may well not realise it has already captured her having sex. Dyer, in a pair of purple boxer shorts, nuzzles her neck. One of the other men urges: "Go on, Kieron my son!" Dyer whispers: "Will you remember this night for the rest of your life?" Soon he jumps on top of her and simulates sex: "Don't you want it!"'

In another scene, the other men have left and the girl clearly believes she is on her own with Dyer. The pair make love. But when the girl sees that the cameraman is in the room again she screams and hides her face in the pillow.

Dyer later said 'sorry' for what he had done. About the film of him, Frank and Rio he said, 'I'd been drinking vodka and Red Bull through the holiday. I hadn't a clue about the exact number of women I had – four or five maybe. For about eight out of ten days I was on the booze.

'We'd all gone out clubbing until about 3am or 4am. I just treated the video as a bit of a laugh. I was aware that the guys had an old camcorder. After I was filmed having sex with the girl, I went up to another one of our mates who was sleeping with a girl. I admit I got my bits out and went, "Whey Hey!" It was a pretty immature thing to do, but we'd all had a few drinks and no one was offended. It was only a joke.

'I remember one of the lads saying, "We've got a bit of footage." It was a mad holiday and we were all a bit naive.'

Naive? Such pursuits for a 'good time', unhappily, have, become part of the public perception of the seedier side of football. Which is why the Frank, Rio and Kieron Dyer video will be reprised in future discussions and documentaries about the dark side of football. It's on the record. It's recorded. Naive? It's probably not the word.

Neil 'Razor' Ruddock went into the jungle for *I'm A Celebrity Get Me Out of Here* with Jordan and George Best's former wife Alex in 2004. He was one of Frank's friends at West Ham in the late 1990s, the leader of the going-out gang, who has been involved with more well-upholstered blondes and booze than most. He offered these thoughts: 'Put any red-blooded, heterosexual male in a room filled with scantily dressed women, fill the bloke with booze, tell the women you're a footballer earning £10,000 a week... it's a recipe for disaster.'

Bruce Goodison's Channel 4 programme *Sex, Footballers and Videotape* will be seen again and again. He was astonished by the results of his investigation into the game, 'An agent told me he had organised fourteen girls' abortions for his footballer clients over six years. Another told me about a London escort agency which had arranged women for almost a dozen footballers at £300 an hour. More shockingly, I discovered incidents of orgies, "gang bangs" or "roasting" involving players from at least half the clubs in the Premiership.

'One girl told me about a former England player who has three cameras – all professionally fitted – hidden in his wardrobe. He keeps a video library of his conquests. There is the incident in Cyprus involving England players Kieron Dyer, Rio Ferdinand and Frank Lampard having consensual sex with a group of girls. "A friend" of the star filmed the romp and it was shown – for the first time on national television – at the start of *Sex, Videotape And Footballers*.

'I felt that it was important to include the footage along with real news archive and newspaper headlines, to remind viewers that the drama is based on the sleazy underbelly of modern football. One of the most disturbing factors to emerge from my research was that so many girls seemed to be complicit in the footballers' appalling behaviour. They, too, are incredibly casual about sex. I met one lap dancer from the Midlands who had slept with a number of local players; another girl from the North who had slept with half her local team. Some didn't enjoy the experience, but liked telling their friends about it. Sex with one or more footballers was a badge of honour.'

Yet it is the girls who usually end up paying the price for such behaviour. The players, too, if they are found out. And Frank was, in the most public way possible. He would do a tremendous amount to wipe out this stain on his character, but it is the video more than the fading memory that will always haunt him.

Chapter Nine

Claret and Blood

'West Ham had been my life since I started
training with them as an eight-year-old.'

FRANK LAMPARD, JULY 2001

'They've got the sack.' They're the words Frank's
mother Pat rushed at him when he walked in the front
door. His father and uncle were out of West Ham as of 9
May 2001. That's the day Harry Redknapp went into a
meeting with his club's chairman Terry Brown. Redknapp
had no idea that the confrontation would end with the
dismantling of a pivotal part of the Hammers' history. It
began, like many disasters, with a small incident.
Redknapp had agreed a new four-year contract with West
Ham, but the club wanted more negotiations.

He then did an interview with a fan magazine in which
he made an offhand remark about the chairman's
arithmetic in regards to the funds brought in by the sale
of Rio Ferdinand to Leeds. Later, Harry revealed, 'The
chairman read it. He reads all the fanzines, looks at
everything on the Internet. And he took the hump. So the

71

following week after we'd beaten Southampton on the Saturday, I walked in to see about my contract and he says, "I'm not happy with you, Harry, I'm going to call it a day."

'I said, "OK. If that's how you feel. I've got two years left on my contract. You'd better make sure you sort me out." And that was that. Shame. I got on well with Terry Brown.

'I never felt sorry for myself, although I did for Frank [Senior]. He [Brown] said, "Frank goes with you." And I said, "No. He goes with West Ham. He's more West Ham than you'll ever be."'

Much bravado but, in the end, Harry Redknapp's run at the club was all over. As was the Lampard legacy. At that moment it seemed Frank was going to join Rio at Leeds for a fee of around £12 million. Yet, there were rumours of other offers from Aston Villa. And Chelsea. Everything was complicated. And, of course, much of it was personal – not just business.

Frank's consigliere, his agent Steve Kuttner, told the *Sunday Mirror* newspaper on 13 May 2001, 'Frank's situation is untenable – how can he kick another ball for the club after what has happened? He has just watched his uncle and his father leave the club. It doesn't take a genius to work out he's extremely upset and sees no future for himself there.'

The newspaper reported that Kuttner alluded to assurances that West Ham had previously given to Frank. It was a pickle. Whichever way looked at it.

Frank later recalled, 'My family were involved and the East End is strong on that. I just couldn't go on playing for West Ham. In these special circumstances I think that is both acceptable and understandable. We talked about it, the family and me, and I discussed the possibilities with my agent Steve Kuttner. I feel emotional and I guess I always will when I think about the sackings.'

Of his father and uncle he said, 'I know people say, "They'll be all right – they can look after themselves." But it's a shock no matter who it happens to. Pride is a big factor. To suddenly find yourself on the outside isn't easy.'

Frank said that he talked to his father every day at that time. He said his father was being realistic and added, 'He's hurting but he's strong. I didn't even know it was even a possibility. I knew nothing about it. I hadn't a clue and that made it more of a shock. I had gone to my mum's and as I walked through the door she just blurted out, "They've got the sack."

'That's the way I found out. It was a terrible experience, the sort of thing that colours your own opinion on whether or not you want to be around the club. West Ham has been my life, basically, since I started training with them when I was eight years old. I have always been ambitious enough to want to move on to something bigger, a club where I could have a better chance of winning things. In a way they forced the decision, but I am sure it would have come anyway. It was a matter of time. I had been linked with Leeds and joining Rio at Elland Road and also with Aston Villa and Chelsea...'

Frank met with Claudio Ranieri at Stamford Bridge. He was impressed. He thought this was a terrific opening. And he wanted to be part of it. The commentators had him going to join Rio at Leeds, but he said, 'Everyone seemed to take it for granted I would go to Leeds because Rio was there, but they were wrong.

'When Rio left and I saw the success he was having then I did feel a bit of what I suppose you could call professional jealousy. But just because something suited him didn't mean it would be the same for me. I wanted a big club and Chelsea are massive. It would have to be a club with ambition – and Chelsea are certainly that.'

Had he only known then of the upcoming Russian revolution. Yet, you make your own luck by being brave. But his attitude was consistent with what was to come: 'It was important to understand what the manager saw in me and expected from me. With Chelsea I would be surrounded by world-class players in a squad that was vastly experienced.

'Chelsea was the future...'

The Upton Park Graduates on 5 January 2005

RIO FERDINAND (Manchester United):
Joined Leeds from West Ham in November 2000 for a fee of £18 million.

In July 2002, Manchester United paid £30 million to take him to Old Trafford.

GLEN JOHNSON (Chelsea):
Was a West Ham first-team player for only sixteen games before Chelsea hired him in July 2003 for £6 million. Aged twenty he's already made his England debut as a substitute, playing right-back.

CLARET AND BLOOD

JOE COLE (Chelsea):
Three weeks after Chelsea bought Glen Johnson, they paid
£6.6 million for Joe Cole, another England international.
The twenty-three-year-old midfielder has flourished under
Jose Mourinho.

JERMAIN DEFOE (Tottenham):
West Ham spotted his Jimmy Greaves-like touches when
he was a teenager at Charlton and took him to Upton
Park. Spurs got involved in February 2004 and Defoe has
since made his England debut.

MICHAEL CARRICK (Tottenham):
West Ham sold him to Tottenham at the start of the
2004–05 season for £2.75 million. Carrick, twenty-three, is
expected to build on his two England caps.

Part Two
The Blues

'English football has grown up a lot since my arrival.
When you bring in something good from other countries it will
always raise the level of competition. Frank Lampard is a
great example. When he arrived at Chelsea I could see straight
away he had great potential. Every day he pushed himself, but it
has really helped that he's had great players around him.
Today, young English players can live out their fantasies playing
alongside World Cup winners.'

GIANFRANCO ZOLA, FEBRUARY 2005

Chapter Ten

Singing the Blues

'I'm a London person. I love London. I'm close to my
family here, and, when I spoke to Chelsea, they sold the
club to me in such a way I couldn't say no.'

FRANK LAMPARD, 18 NOVEMBER 2001

The exceptional and exciting Gianfranco Zola recalls
the arrival of Claudio Ranieri to Chelsea with some
bemusement. Forget the football. There were some
interesting cultural lessons to be learned as Zola, the one-
time footballing partner of Diego Maradona, who you feel
one day wants to return to west London, explained,
'When he first came, he handled the players like he would
in Italy or Spain. I had to explain that in England he
would have to be more accommodating. You cannot sit on
players twenty-four hours a day. In Italy and Spain you
control everything they do. In England it is different. You
have to give them more space.'

And Frank was looking for space. His own space. In
September 1999, Chelsea could only find room for one
Englishman, Dennis Wise, in their starting line-up against
Milan. A couple of years on, Frank, the East End boy, was

edging Wise out. He completed his £11 million transfer across London from West Ham to Chelsea on 14 June 2001.

It was a wrench, no matter how ill the feelings were about what happened at West Ham with his father and uncle. 'I was told Rio wouldn't be sold and, I was very upset when he went. Then the manager went. Things were happening that I didn't like and when the chance came for me to move, it appealed to me. I always dreamed of playing for a massive club.

'The treatment and criticism of them was very unfair. Look at the youth system and the Academy Harry put in place. Rio went for £18 million. I was £11 million. And there was Joe Cole, Michael Carrick and Jermain Defoe. Without Harry and my dad those players wouldn't be there. I remember Rio coming round to our house when he was fourteen and Dad getting him to sign. Without little things like that, the club would never have done so well with young kids.

'Harry took the club a long way and deserved credit, not criticism. I had the chance to go to Leeds. I'm a London person. I love London. I'm close to my family here, and, when I spoke to Chelsea, they sold the club to me in such a way I couldn't say no.'

Frank says the first great difference he noticed between West Ham and Chelsea was that of expectation. The management, the players, the fans, all expected great things. 'We were talking at the start of the season about winning the League and the UEFA Cup, whereas at West Ham we may have said, "Can we get into Europe?"

'At Chelsea we just didn't hope to do well, but were

expected to.' Frank was also impressed by his surroundings. 'The minute I walked into the stadium, the feel of the place got to me. What with the hotel on the site and the forty-five thousand capacity. It feels like a big club. No disrespect to West Ham, but you're training with world-class players. Just watching and working with them, you can't help but learn. It feels like an honour to train with them.'

These early days with Chelsea convinced him he had made the right choice. 'Chelsea was the right move,' he said time and time again. And it was. His 'dream move' put Frank with the big boys. And for all the correct reasons. His talent. His dedication. And his potential.

Yet only weeks after he made the move, the atrocities of 11 September 2001 happened. It affected the world and also Frank, in a much less tragic, but pertinent to him, way. He had joined Chelsea with an old-world heritage. Suddenly, the New World went berserk. For much of that world the simple values had utterly changed.

But what got into Frank's head? For there were to be unfortunate headlines 'Up West'. The day after the New York attacks, Frank was out and about with his friends and upset American visitors to London. This is how, in brief, the problem was reported on 23 September 2001: 'Their football game had been cancelled as a mark of respect for the thousands massacred in America only twenty-four hours earlier – but four of Chelsea's top stars had no intention of mourning the dead. Instead the swaggering Premiership players went on an astonishing five-hour booze-fuelled rampage in the wake of the world's worst terrorist attack – stripping, laughing and vomiting in front of shocked and grieving Americans in a Heathrow hotel bar.

'The drunken stars – including England Under-21 players Frank Lampard, Jody Morris and John Terry – sneered and hurled abuse as numbed customers watched the disaster unfolding on television.

'Heathrow's Post House hotel was full of weeping Americans and Britons – stranded as transatlantic flights were grounded and frantically trying to phone New York and Washington for news of loved ones. They couldn't believe their eyes as the players' appalling behaviour unfolded before them. Today we can reveal that the players' loathsome antics have landed them fines totalling more than £100,000 from outraged Chelsea bosses who listened aghast as *News of the World* investigators revealed the evidence against them.

'Post House manager Vishal Ramkisson told us, "They were utterly disgusting. They just didn't seem to care about what had happened. We had a lot of Americans here and were simply trying to comfort them in their hour of need. Meanwhile, these men were laughing and joking, taking off their clothes and abusing our guests. One of them was walking around laughing with everything hanging out, while on television there were crying firemen searching for bodies. It was sick."

'The group, who also included Icelandic international Eidur Gudjohnsen, twenty-three, and twenty-nine-year-old former Chelsea defender Frank Sinclair, ended their foul day by going berserk at a bowling alley, scattering frightened customers as they slid down the lanes head first towards the pins. The players began their day of shame at Chelsea's training ground near Heathrow Airport on Wednesday, 12 September, after hearing that night's UEFA Cup tie at home to Bulgarian side Levski Sofia had been called off.

'There Gudjohnsen, Lampard, twenty-three, and Terry, twenty, were met by pal Sinclair, now with Leicester City. When they left the Harlington ground they went to the nearby White Hart for an hour before rolling into the Red Lion at 3.30pm. Red Lion landlord Joe O'Brien revealed, "The whole group was out of order, they'd had well enough to drink so I asked them to leave. They were upsetting other people in the bar."

'Regular Dominic Jenkins added, "Nobody could believe it, especially after what had happened in America. They obviously didn't care who saw them drunk. I saw Lampard, Morris, Terry, Gudjohnsen and Sinclair sticking it away. Gudjohnsen was hammered and shouting out swear words. They started throwing peanuts. When they got outside they stripped one other lad who was with them – he wasn't a player – and left him naked at a bus stop."

'Driver Warren Lunnon confirmed, "They were all hurling abuse at people and chucking things at the landlord. They were asked to be quiet but started piping up again. Lampard, Morris and Sinclair went out and urinated in a bin in the street."

'The group then lurched to another pub, The Wheatsheaf, but the landlord turned them away. So they staggered on up the street to the Post House hotel teeming with grieving, stunned Americans. It was 5.30pm.

Reception manager Emma Migheli said, "The Americans were desperately worried and waiting to fly home to get news of loved ones."

'There one of the players took off his trousers and pants and exposed himself to a packed bar watching television footage of the tragedy across the Atlantic. Hotel manager Mr Ramkisson said, "Where was their respect and dignity? As soon as they sat down things got out of hand. They began pestering some young ladies who were in the bar. The ladies were very upset, so I went over and had a word. I could see these men were completely drunk. I asked one, Frank Sinclair, if they would leave because they were frightening guests. But he said they were having a good time. One of the players had his pants down and knew 'it' was out and was walking around like that. Guests were disgusted at their behaviour, so I asked them to leave again. Eventually they left, but only after I threatened to call the police."

'Tracy King, who worked behind the bar that day, added, "They were disgusting. I didn't know they were footballers, but lots of people told me afterwards exactly who they were. They were swearing a lot, upsetting people, and one of them pulled his underwear down at least three times. I could see it all and the restaurant was packed. People asked to be moved to other tables. Other guests were trying to concentrate on the news on the television, but they couldn't. One of the players downed a pint of lager and then vomited it back all over the floor."'

The article was clearly upsetting after his wonderful transfer from West Ham to Chelsea. And what about his

England hopes? Frank, who has shown exemplary public behaviour ever since, told the forgiving Joe Lovejoy in the *Sunday Times*, on 18 November 2001, 'There's a lot of things I could tell you about the whole day, but I'm not going into that. Let's just say that a lot of things people said happened didn't happen. None of the players who were involved are horrible people. We have just been painted that way, but it isn't like that.'

Given Frank's attitude, Mr Lovejoy didn't pursue, in print anyway, the matter any further. Like Tony Blair, he moved on, drew a line under it, so to speak. He wrote, 'Lampard preferred to look forward...'

And, in truth, he has. Later, in December 2004, he reflected on what had happened. He said he was happy to say 'sorry' and he admitted being 'loud'. He says he and the other players were 'all in it together'. Certainly, the reports of the incident contradicted the image of Frank in 2005, but he was younger. And he knows it. He said of the aftermath of the incident: 'My mum and dad both said to me, "If you don't learn from this, you're stupid."

'Looking back, I don't think I was ever flash. I've never been one to chuck cash around [like father like son say some of his father's East End friends] and show off. My parents kept my feet on the ground. I think my biggest fault was naivety. You're there to be seen, everywhere you go, everything you do. It's not like my mates, who can do whatever they want and nobody knows. Your values change when you get older and I'm more mature now.'

As a result of the incident, Chelsea decided that its three England Under-21 players (Lampard, Terry and Morris) and international Gudjohnsen should be fined two weeks' wages –£100,00 in total. The money was donated to the fund for bereaved families in America. The club's managing director Colin Hutchinson said, 'Their behaviour was totally out of order, but there is no way that the players went out, in any shape or form, to insult or abuse anyone.

'They were categorical that in no way had they intended to insult any individuals and said they certainly didn't abuse anyone. They were loud between themselves but they, like everyone at the club, have been as hurt and moved by what has happened in the United States as anyone else.'

But what about England? Frank had a bad day at Spurs and was sent off on 16 September 2001. A dozen days later, he discovered that he had been left out of Sven-Goran Eriksson's plans for England's game against Greece. Eriksson, sensitive to the world situation, made it extravagantly clear that players who stepped out of line would not be part of his World Cup plans. 'My players have to be professional. I agree with that 200 per cent.

'We are England. We are not a small country. We are one of the biggest in the world. That means we have to play well and have to conduct ourselves well and do everything well. You can't hope to win the World Cup in 2002 or 2006 if you accept anything less. I always make my selection decisions on footballing grounds. But, if a player isn't playing well or not doing well on or off the pitch, that has to do with football. All of us have a big responsibility if we want to be part of the England senior team. Millions of young people are looking at us as heroes when we are playing well. We must live up to that, whatever we do.'

But Frank had something to keep him warm. On the tape of his answerphone was the voice of Sven-Goran Eriksson saying, 'You'll be back.'

Eriksson had kicked him out of the World Cup qualifier against Greece, but those answerphone messages were an endorsement: 'Thanks for the part you had in helping us qualify for the World Cup.' And the other: 'I'm leaving you out this time, but you're still in contention, still involved...'

In all the communications between them, Sven-Goran Eriksson never accused Frank of any wrongdoing. Yet, Frank paid his share of the fine. He also achieved the dubious honour of becoming the first player dropped by England on non-footballing grounds since Rio Ferdinand was axed by Glenn Hoddle on the eve of the game with Moldova in September 1997, following his drink-drive conviction. Eriksson's general view is this: 'I try to be very strict when it comes to the general behaviour of players. If a player breaks my rules, on or off the field, he faces the consequences. But it is off the pitch where I have rules I am even more strict about. I am particularly hard on drinking, partying or nightclubbing. I always take action against those who put their own interests ahead of the team. They only destroy the whole structure. When I was younger, I used to punish players by putting them on the bench. But I came to realise that I was only punishing myself. So, what I do now is never pick players I feel are not able to fit in with my rules – either physically or mentally.'

Yet, in the middle of all the controversy, he said of Frank, 'The door is always open. It does not mean that life is finished, absolutely not. I do not think Frank let himself or the country down. I think he is very professional and a good player. All of us are young at some stage. Life goes on. I picked the squad to play Greece, but it doesn't mean the same players will be in the next squad. The new generation of players is much more conscious of what to eat and what to drink to keep in shape, and the club managers here have been doing a very good job on this issue. I say to my players, quite simply, that we are here to play football, not to drink. If you want to drink, then just go home.'

Frank, being Frank of course, knuckled down. There was only one goal – the World Cup squad. He got some of his inspiration from Rio Ferdinand, who called Frank with his encouragement and good wishes. In March 2005, Ferdinand was more practical voting for his friend as the Football Association's Footballer of the Year to the detriment of his fellow defender John Terry. At that time Rio had vowed to curb the excessive lifestyle and Eriksson warned that other Premiership players must do the same if they wanted to be part of his World Cup campaign.

The much-liked Zola also forged some thoughts on the episode: 'The matter belongs to the past. Everybody makes mistakes, but they have paid the price and it was a heavy one in financial terms. They know what they've done. They didn't mean to cause anybody any offence but obviously they did. Now they have paid with their own money and it will go to a good cause. The players have been reprimanded and we have had a chat about things as players.

'We are responsible for things like this and they know that now. They didn't want to cause any problem, it is as simple as that. Nobody lives their life perfectly and even I made mistakes when I was younger, but I didn't have anybody taking photographs of me. The important thing is not to think of them doing what they did deliberately. They realise what they have done and they have taken the responsibility for it. They now know not to do things like that in the future.'

And for Frank at Chelsea there was Claudio Ranieri, who was so impressed by his box-to-box style of play that he pledged himself to make Frank the best midfielder in the game.

Chapter Eleven

The Italian Job

'They don't get kicked as hard because there is more
surveillance. In the old days, we had people who were
playing with hairline fractures of the leg.'

JEFF POWELL, FEBRUARY 2005

Frank and Chelsea dovetailed. The players, the club, the
atmosphere? Whatever. Sometimes the magic works,
sometimes it doesn't. And no one ever truly knows why.
The magic happened. He was the first English signing
for Claudio Ranieri and that was the beginning of a
beautiful friendship.

Frank's message was clear. He had moved to Chelsea
because he wanted to improve as a player and expand his
horizons. The better the people, the better he would
become. He recalled, 'When I trained with England for the
first time after Rio joined Leeds, I could see an
improvement in him – not just as a player but as a person
and in his strength of character. I was impressed by how
much he had come on by playing in the Champions
League and being made captain of Leeds. It adds another
string to your bow.'

And Frank was up for playing a 12-string guitar. There were many around him then – and more now – who could feel the burning ambition within him. Frank Lampard had a point to make. And he was going to make it.

Mr Freud and lots of others might have drawn conclusions as to the source of the motivation, but those of us on the amateur psychological couch can only present the evidence. For Frank didn't leave his roots easily, 'I had talks with West Ham about staying, but they didn't last very long. I had a good think about it, but I'd made up my mind. The first I heard of Chelsea's interest was from reading the paper. Chelsea want and need success and I am looking forward to testing myself against the best players in Europe. I think I proved myself at West Ham and I played for England while with them. But I'm sure playing in Europe will give me that extra edge.'

Yet Ronald De Boer of Glasgow Rangers believed Chelsea should have gone for his Dutch club-mate Giovanni van Bronckhorst. When that story got out, there were large headlines. Frank, who was already getting cute at the PR and avoiding own goals in this new high-profile world, responded, 'I was a bit disappointed, but I don't talk about other players. It shows a lack of respect.'

And respect is something Frank had learned and was taking into his new life and career with Chelsea. Jeff Powell, who reported on his father's career and today is one of Britain's most astute and influential sports commentators, explained, 'Let me give you an idea of the change. Johnny Haynes was the first £100-a-week footballer. Of course, John stayed at Fulham his entire senior career, even resisting Tottenham at the end which would have been a bonus for him really. That was the only one that tempted him.

'Anyway £100 a week, which made everyone go "My God" and I thought, What is that today? I thought that with inflation it would now put him at £1,500 a week.

'Today's Johnny Haynes on those precepts would be earning £1,500 a week. Of course, it was considered outrageous at the time that John got £100 a week. The interesting thing about young Frank is that he is one of the few players who plays every game, the same thing as people like his father did. He is considered to be a phenomenon because he just plays every match, whereas everybody else is getting rotated.

'They complain they can't play twice a week, while his father, and all the other guys at West Ham or wherever, from Bobby Moore downwards, were all playing every game, and a lot of those games were played on extremely heavy pitches with a great thumping old ball.

'You weren't looking at nice new technology. You've seen them now; they're like super beach balls. They don't fly off in the air like beach balls do, but they're light to kick and the pitches are all lovely. You don't see games now where they're playing through quagmires, do you?

'This is what stopped them winning World Cups. I think when we went to Japan, the most played player in the Eriksson team for the World Cup had thirty-odd games in the season and a lot of those games were not full games. Well, there were no substitutes back in Frank Senior's day. Bobby Moore, in the season prior to leading us to the only

World Cup we ever won had played sixty-three games. You just got on with it. Young Frank is a bit of a throwback to that really. He's hard work and he plays box to box and he gets his goals and he plays every game, and very rarely comes off.

'Frank [Senior] was a proper professional and he brought his boy up right. Frank had a lot to do with keeping his head straight, there's no question about that. Of course, some of the biggest influences on Frank included people like Moore and Malcolm Allison. Malcolm was a very good thinker on the game. Always trying to be innovative, so Frank Junior's father's peer group was an important, collateral, influence on him.

'Frank took a lot of the principles on which he played the game and lived his social life from Moore, which wasn't bad. Today the players don't turn out for every game, the argument being that the pace of the game means they can't play so often. Well, bullshit, because, basically, with the medical and dietary help, it enables them to do that, that's why the game is quicker. They don't get kicked as hard because there is more surveillance nowadays. We had people who were playing with hairline fractures of the leg in the old days... Frank's attitude towards playing every match is admirable really in a game where they all say they want to play every game, but when they are offered it they don't want to do it.

'When Bobby Moore went to Fulham, Alex Stock said with some surprise, knowing Bobby would be up all night drinking, because he was an insomniac, "It's amazing. Bobby Moore lived the other side of London and who is first into training? Bobby Moore who is out there sweating off any beer he's had the night before, before the others even think about getting in."

'I remember going on holiday with Bobby to South Africa, and he would knock on the door at 7am lively and shout, "Come on, off we go running on the beach."

'His weight didn't change by more than three or four pounds in the off-season. That enabled him to do that.

'You've seen the contrast with Beckham.

'Beckham is supposed to be a product of the new high-tech football society, but unlike Mr Moore, who he likes to think he's the successor to, he turned up fat for Euro 2004. He should have been sent home. He couldn't take his top off because he was always posing around with his shirt off normally and, when he finally did, there was a belly. It was disgraceful. You don't see young Frank do that.

'In the old days you had a much greater mingling. After the games they used to go to the pub with people like myself and we'd hang out and we'd drink. Then, if you wanted to know what was going on about the games during the week, at lunchtime after training we used to go to the cafe in the High Street, and they were all looking at tactics over the egg and bacon. It was a much different way of going about it, but it was a good way in many ways.

'Frank might have come to the conclusion, I don't know whether it's valid or not, that's why he can play every game. That's why he can play football twice a week. That's what he thinks about and gets fit for. He is, from the moment we first saw him, definitely "trained on" as they say in horseracing.

'He didn't look like a world beater; he looked like a good player with some limitations. I mean an honest player, but not God's gift to football. He's obviously really worked at it to improve his game. He must be applying whatever is between his ears to think about the game and how to be better at it, plus practising his skills.

'David Beckham's saving grace was always the training. Alex Ferguson tells us how many times in a week he would look up from his office at the training ground and it was getting dark and would say, "What is he still doing out there practising free-kicks?" He used to have to go and drag him off the pitch.

'Beckham finally lost it for a lot of us when he turned up unfit. If you don't turn up in shape you let everybody down. He's looking a bit fitter again now. He's obviously feeling the squeeze. The heat's on him, and his face is a bit more gaunt again. He was really podgy for a time. It was shameful really.

'That's not true about Lampard because he's always nicely turned out. Wayne Rooney's the only fellow who overshadowed him in Euro 2004. Frank, if you were looking, was the one who'd really come on. Frank is doing more for Chelsea in 2005 than young Wayne is doing for Manchester United.

'Frank wasn't standing the world on its ear at his age either, but perhaps it was a bit out of kilter that he got overshadowed so much by the Rooney explosion. That's where he consolidated himself as a player, I thought.

'Of course, what he's had to do at Chelsea is prove himself and retain his place, and in order to do so against that competition you've got to be better than them by some distance. Yes, he cost money, but he's had to see off the big glamour foreign stars. There was a lot of the talk about "I'll knuckle down and find my place and my future", but he's actually done it.

'That's the other thing about Frank. You don't think he's going to lose the plot. He knows what's brought his game on. And there's a lot of money about. It's astonishing really. I don't think his dad is one who resents the big money for the youngsters now. Frank [Senior] doesn't go around saying, "Well, we should have got it", but then I suppose if you've got a kid bringing home that kind of dosh...

'Frank Senior watches his son a lot. He goes whenever he can to watch him, and he's a good counsellor for him. He's a very sensible guy, Frank Senior. Oh yes, businesses and what have you. He didn't just think, I'll worry about it when the time comes, he was trying to sort it. Frank's very bright and he's got a good head on his shoulders, and Frank Junior has inherited a bit of that. Also, the other comparison is that Frank Senior grew up when West Ham really did educate players.

'Frank Junior would have got the benefit of his dad's exposure to the education that West Ham used to be, but then had to get out because they weren't doing it any more and clearly the experience of playing at Chelsea with world-class players was better for him.'

Chapter Twelve
King of the Road

'Memories in football tend to be very short.
Speculation is the spice of our job.'

CLAUDIO RANIERI, 17 OCTOBER 2004

Claudio Ranieri joined Chelsea in September 2000, in the aftermath of the departure of Gianluca Vialli. The management turnover – Glen Hoddle, Ruud Gullit – was, it seemed, a permanent way of life at Stamford Bridge where there had been nine managers in just twice that number of years.

Pasta-buff Ranieri, surprised as anyone by the move, brought his own special skills and personality to the job. It was understandable that he should become close to Gianfranco Zola, whom he had known as a young player at Napoli. Of course, he became known as the 'Tinkerman', but he never had a chance to play any role in the departure, after seven seasons, of Zola from Chelsea to his Sardinian home and Cagilari. 'I really wanted Franco to stay, but he and the club could not agree over wages. I wasn't surprised by what happened – Chelsea should have made more of an effort to keep him, but they were involved in other matters. They lost a great player and a great ambassador. We made friends because of him and I think he must have been the most loved Italian in England. His loyalty, generosity and technical skills were all put at the disposal of the club and he was a vital leader in the dressing room.'

Ranieri watched John Terry take on that role. Terry has his own West Ham connection – he grew up on the same housing estate in Barking as Bobby Moore. He brought Terry in for Frank Leboeuf and astutely predicted that the tall, strong and most determined young man would develop into the Tony Adams role for Chelsea – and England. He was impressed by the individual self-belief shown by Terry and by Frank, two of his favourite Chelsea 'sons'.

One clued-up commentator called the emergence of the duo 'Claudio Ranieri's greatest achievement' at Chelsea. Ranieri was – and is – certainly fond of them. 'They have a great spirit and that is so important, so vital in building confidence – in winning games. They show English strength, character. A team should always reflect the character of the nation.

'It was never in my character – and I think I have a good character – to say we will win this or win that. I just went out and tried to do that with the team. It takes time to develop a team. Time.'

But there was always immense pressure to win shiny silverware for the Chelsea boardroom's walnut cabinets. In his initial seasons, Ranieri brought in Frank as well as

KING OF THE ROAD

William Gallas, Nikola Jokanovic, Jesper Gronkjaer, Emmanuel Petit and Boudewijn Zenden: Frank was the pick of the litter.

In his book *Claudio Ranieri, Proud Man Walking* (Collins Willow, 2004), which Chelsea insisted by contract in vetting, the man the East End lad found in charge when he arrived at Chelsea said, 'Among his other considerable qualities, Frank has one that cannot be taught: a predatory instinct that ensures he is always in the right place at the right moment to take advantage of sharp chances. He is almost unique in this.'

Ranieri (his Chelsea programme notes always ended with 'together with all our hearts') says speculation is the spice of his job, a rich factor in much that goes on behind the scenes. During his entrancing time with Chelsea, there was always talk of bringing new stars to the club. As the months ticked away and the 'events' happened, the gossip sometimes became quite frenetic, spicy: Thierry Henry (£50 million offer), David Beckham and Ronaldo (joint offer of £70 million), Michael Owen (£25 million), Roberto Carlos (£50 million) and Raul (£71 million). At one point Ranieri was quizzed about Wayne Rooney and he gave that familiar shrug: 'If I say I'm not interested, you won't believe me.'

Nevertheless, he had more of a track record with the truth than Tony Blair in that area. Ranieri was liked by the fans and the players, but did his affability blunt any killer instinct? The announcement of his move to London was given a deadpan précis in the Italian press: 'Claudio Ranieri was born in Rome in 1951. After an unspectacular

101

playing career with Roma, he took up the coaching reins at Cagliari before moving on to Fiorentina, Valencia and Atletico Madrid. He quit Atletico in March 2000 and took over as manager at Chelsea later that summer.'

Yet, the gregarious and good-natured Ranieri became someone the nation took to their hearts, which was a surprise after his first reception at Chelsea, when thousands of fans shamelessly chanted the name of the club's previous manager, Gianluca Vialli, from the stands.

It didn't help that Ranieri's English was not great. The newspapers could have fun with that at the Press conferences. He was easily lampooned – mercilessly he became 'Clownio', the Inspector Clouseau of the Premiership. Much was made of the fact that in the early months he had to communicate with the players through an interpreter.

Endearingly, he admitted how tough it was with another language – even after his tenure at Chelsea: 'How is it possible that I don't speak English very well? I took lessons three days a week for two years, but with the work it was very hard.'

He became a joy on the sports pages with remarks about his team like: 'They showed good stamina and good vitamins.' He may even have invented his nickname, the Tinkerman, as a way of lowering criticism of his chaotic transfer deals and his constant changing of the starting XI. Always immaculately groomed, favouring sharp suits for games and tweeds and loose-fitting cords when off-duty, he has the solid physique of a former defender so in contrast with his soft manner.

KING OF THE ROAD

On the touchline he ran an emotional alphabet shouting, screaming, slapping his thighs in frustration, remonstrating with the bench or, his set piece, exploding in a volcano of words. In London he drove a Ferrari, often accompanying his wife Rosanna to antique fairs. She owns two shops in Rome selling 1950s furniture. They lived well in a Fulham home. Ranieri took his work home with him and of Rosanna he said, 'She suffers a lot for me. She has given me a lot of support, but she is not a football fan. My wife likes to buy the highest quality. I like quality footballers, she likes quality furniture.'

He was born in Testaccio, an area of Rome just south of the Circus Maximus, where his father owned a butcher's shop. He adored football from the beginning. He learned to play in the inter-parish ties between the churches of San Saba and San Anselmo. 'There was good fighting there. Fantastic.'

His three older brothers followed their father into the butcher business, but Claudio was going to play football for Roma. At eighteen he achieved his dream, but his tough, strong play did not offer enough to offset his other abilities. He was not a team regular. He went south to the Serie B team Catanzaro, where he met and married Rosanna, a local girl. In 1981, their daughter Claudia was born. He continued to play until 1986, transferring first to Catania and then to Palermo, where, at the age of thirty-five, he decided he wanted to be a manager. At a course held by the Italian Football Association, he was told that being a manager was like parachuting – 'Sometimes the 'chute doesn't open and you splatter on the ground.'

He enjoyed management. 'As a manager, win or lose, you are responsible for everything. I liked the pressure.' He spent a decade being noticed, but not advantaged, until he found the glories of Spain and Valencia in 1997. When he was appointed manager, the club was bottom of La Liga and not getting much decent change from the lavishly remunerated stars like the Brazilian Romario and Ariel Ortega from Argentina. Ortega shaped up, but Romario did not survive his intimate talk with Ranieri.

In two seasons Ranieri laid the foundations for the club's run to the Champions League final. Then he stumbled. He accepted an offer from Atletico Madrid, where he clashed with Jesus Gil, a wealthy patron. Within a couple of months the club was on its way to relegation, in judicial administration and Gil was jailed. Ranieri resigned and spent the next six months out of the game kicking his well-heeled heels.

But then came September 2000. 'Colin Hutchinson [Chelsea's managing director] invited me to come and see Chelsea because they had just sacked Vialli four days earlier. The day after, I was asked if I wanted to work with the players. I said, "Yes, OK, I am very grateful."'

And he looked around for friends. He found one, of course, with Zola, but also with Frank, who arrived at Chelsea a few months later at the same time as the acceptance and emergence of the team's new manager. Ranieri says he liked Frank's attitude, which was that he would do whatever it took, however many hours of training, to be in that Chelsea team for every game. That's the way it worked.

Look into my eyes! Frank's dad in his playing days for West Ham and England.
The Lampards share sparkling eyes and fabulous football footwork.

That's my boy! His uncle was the manager and his father was a West Ham coach but Frank's talent made a mockery of the nepotism chants.

Above: Frank Lampard exchanges gifts with Erhan Albayrak of Turkey before a European under-21 match.

Right: Young Frank in action showing the Hammers' fans that he was a serious star in the making – another of Upton Park's great graduates.

Teenaged Rio Ferdinand came to tea at the Lampards – and signed on for West Ham where he and Frank became great mates. Rio's departure was the catalyst for Frank's move to Chelsea.

he Tinkerman, Claudio Ranieri, who spotted Lamps's potential and took him
om the East End to the West End and Stamford Bridge.

Above: How sweet it is – Frank celebrates another spectacular goal for Chelsea.

Below: Frank emerged in 2005 as the post-match spokesman for the team; his thoughts always calm, collected and quietly presented.

Flying high – and off to another monumental Champions League encounter.

Jose Mourinho knew the way for Frank Lampard – the manager and his prized
player celebrate another victory after their outstanding season together.

KING OF THE ROAD

It was no wonder Ranieri adopted him and, in turn, John Terry. His motivation was to create winners, but he was also aware that he was working for such an historic English football club. For Ranieri it was a marvellous adventure. In Italy, the newspapers reported how he had changed his hairstyle and his spectacles – he was a person always ready to wrap himself in a new country, a new identity. It was Ken Bates who gave him the job in September 2000, and the owner said then, 'The team are very disciplined and that comes from leadership from the top. When's the last time you heard him criticise a referee? When's the last time you heard him suggest he was temporarily blind? When's the last time you heard him slag off another opponent or manager?'

Ranieri did not control only himself. He is of the old school, a man who insists on complete command of the dressing room and he was never put off by the thought of making himself unpopular.

Jimmy Floyd Hasselbaink, during a rough time at Stamford Bridge, gave some sharp thoughts: 'I don't like it when, on the evening before a game, the manager storms into your hotel room and takes all the wires out of the television set because he's afraid you'll be watching it all night.'

'He was a very tough manager to work with,' said Irishman Damien Duff, adding, 'He made it really intense for us every single day in training. There was absolutely no let-up, whereas at Blackburn we just had five-a-side kickabouts.'

Frank admired the work ethic and thrived on it.

SUPER FRANK

One good-natured Italian journalist suggested Ranieri lived up to Machiavelli's mandate for a prince by being a fox and a lion. Events, including Russian bears and so on, would require Ranieri to master all the cunning and ferocity he could.

Throughout, he was always a gentleman.

Chapter Thirteen

When in Rome

'What Alex Ferguson has with Roy Keane
I maybe have in Frank Lampard.'

CLAUDIO RANIERI, NOVEMBER 2003

In his new Chelsea world, the Claudio culture was another eye-opener for Frank. The manager made it clear to his players: 'This is a new era for Chelsea. Whoever understands this rests with us. If they don't understand, I'm sorry. Instead of being with us they can rest.'

Frank, of course, got the message. He developed in Claudio's reign and, after some years of being on a management seesaw, there appeared to be stability at Chelsea. Ranieri said he told Frank when they first met that his attacking game worked well. Yet, he had to improve his defensive play. Ranieri pointed out in his autobiography that Frank didn't always please him: 'He would follow a natural instinct that prompted him to get involved in attacking moves, and his sense of timing was perfect for it, but he made me cross sometimes, because this exposed the midfield and, as I explained to him, if he was forever darting forward, he would never be able to count on the element of surprise, which, in his case, could be decisive.'

Ranieri said in 2003 that when he used Frank 'now and again out on the right, he would continue to drift into the middle, upsetting the team's balance'. But by 2004 he added, 'With a string of phenomenal performances and goals, he forced me, gratifyingly, to play him in central midfield. Now my only problem was a different one: finding a way to rest him. Almost all observers were united in the view that he was the most vital player, not only of our team but indeed of the whole Premiership, in these first few months of the season.

'I agreed with them and it was no coincidence, in statistical terms, he totalled more minutes on the pitch than anyone else in the squad for the season. I knew I needed to rest him now and again, but with all the injuries to our midfielders conspiring against me as well, how could I leave him out?'

His feelings towards Lampard were revealed further when he wrote following the Chelsea v. Lazio game in the Champions League at Stamford Bridge on 22 October 2003: 'After eight minutes of the second half we had turned it around (from 0–1) with two genuine stunners from Lampard and Mutu. After the interval I saw the character of my team: a phenomenal Lampard (by now the norm) and Veron at his best since donning the blue of Chelsea.'

Ranieri packed his book with praise for Frank and noted, in particular, the Blackburn v. Chelsea game at Ewood Park on 1 February 2004, which Chelsea won 3–2: 'In this game, as in others, a decisive contribution was made by Frank Lampard, who was playing behind the strikers for the first time in the season. He scored two and was close to a hat-trick.'

At home on 27 March 2004 when Chelsea played Wolves at home and won 5–2, the manager said of his adopted 'son', 'A special day for Lampard – this was his 100th consecutive Premier League appearance. He scored one of his "super goals".' There was never any question as to whether or not Ranieri was a Frank Lampard super-fan.

Throughout his reign, Ranieri never lost his concentration for the team – and much was going on around him. And beneath him. The foundations at Chelsea were being resoundly shaken. Business-wise, Chelsea were in a financial quagmire. Ken Bates was floundering. The club needed new training facilities – a new start in life after nearly 100 years. Roman Abramovich bought the club in the summer of 2003 when Ranieri and his team were driving forward.

Actually, Ranieri was driving through France with his wife when he heard the news in a close-to-midnight telephone call from Trevor Birch of Chelsea to his mobile phone. Whatever emotions he felt, he should have been the happiest football manager on the planet. Four days later, he was sitting face to face with Abramovich, the new owner of Chelsea Football Club, who gave him more than £100 million to spend on buying a dream team.

Abramovich, quiet but determined, wanted a collection of stars who would pitch Chelsea into the stellar league of Manchester United and Real Madrid. Ranieri wanted a team. There was an underlying clash over stars and hard-working players but, for the moment, Ranieri was in. As he said earlier, he had no illusions about Roman Abramovich's desires: 'I knew Roman didn't want me to drive the car, he wanted Schumacher. And he was looking for Schumacher.'

From then on there was much speculation. Would Sven-Goran Eriksson be in charge? It was a constant debate for all concerned at the club and Frank's friend, Eidur Gudjohnsen, recalled what went on after the takeover: 'I was on holiday when I first heard that Roman Abramovich had bought Chelsea. My dad telephoned me from Iceland to tell me that a super-rich Russian had just taken over the club. It came as a shock to me, as I never thought Ken Bates would sell his shares. As soon as I heard about the extent of Abramovich's wealth I knew there would be many new faces arriving before pre-season training.

'There was uncertainty among the existing players until Abramovich made it clear to us that he only wanted to add to the squad rather than get rid of people. So when we signed Hernan Crespo and Adrian Mutu I didn't feel under threat. I knew I was going to have to be patient and wait for my chance. To be honest, I found it all quite exciting. As a player you want to win things and I felt the new signings could make this possible, especially after we started the season so well. From a personal point of view, it was difficult to sit and watch those early games from the bench, but when you're at a very big club – which is what all the new money made us – you just have to accept it.

'The other thing we had to get used to was Abramovich

coming into the changing room after the game. He doesn't say too much; he just walks around and shakes hands with people. He never tried to interfere with team talks or tried to tell Claudio Ranieri what to do. That's not his job or why he's in there. I just think he wanted to show us that he was interested in the team, that he wanted us to succeed.

'The constant rumours that surrounded Claudio Ranieri, as to whether or not he would be leaving, didn't affect the players too much. We didn't really speak about it. It often got to the point that there was so much speculation and rubbish written that you ended up either ignoring it or laughing about it. If you want to play for a big club and be successful, then press attention and pressure is something that you have to get used to.'

It was Ranieri's dignity amid all the rumours about his future that endeared him to many. He also kept to his own rules: he picked hard-working players, like Frank, who might bond together. 'I wanted players with character. My idea was to create a group, because a team is a group and I wanted everybody to work together.'

Despite the guillotine hovering above him, Ranieri's strategy paid off. The big moment came when they recorded their first victory over Arsenal in six years on 6 April 2004. 'It was a great night for me as I set up the winning goal,' said Gudjohnsen, who added, 'But it is a moment that really stands out for everyone at the club.'

It was, cruel happenstance, also the beginning of the end for Claudio Ranieri at Chelsea. After Wayne Bridge's winning goal at Highbury, the Chelsea fans – always Shedalert to the rumour mill – were chanting that Abramovich couldn't sack Ranieri now. Couldn't he?

Yet Chelsea were now the unexpected favourites to reach the Champions League final – something achieved by only one English club, Manchester United, since 1985.

But there was such a whirlwind of talk around Abramovich and his advisers that the Highbury win was seen by many as just a stay of execution for Ranieri. The manager also seemed to suspect as much, judging by his body language in the post-match interviews. He seemed very uncomfortable and frantically rubbed his nose.

What Ranieri's supporters – the *Sun* proclaimed that Ranieri was 'the most likeable man in football' – did not know was that, on 17 March 2004, Ottmar Hitzfeld, the Bayern Munich coach, said he had been approached by Chelsea. There were stories linking the club to two other exemplar coaches, Fabio Capello and Carlo Ancelotti, culminating, it seems, in Sven-Goran Eriksson's secret assignation.

Ranieri's tears flowed that night at Highbury and he made many lifelong friends that evening. Yes, he was emotional that Chelsea had beaten Arsenal against all the odds and stood on the cusp of an historic European Champions League final. But mostly his tears expressed relief and vindication that, after months of plotting to get rid of him, the then fifty-two-year-old manager was not the 'dead man walking' that the pragmatic pundits said he was. Not yet, anyway.

What had impressed everybody was the way that Ranieri had risen above the sustained efforts to undermine him. These came to a head about two weeks before the triumph at Highbury. It was leaked that Manchester United's former background mastermind Peter Kenyon, now Chelsea's chief executive, had invited the England coach, Sven-Goran Eriksson, for an afternoon-tea meeting to discuss the possibility of him replacing Ranieri.

It was cat and mouse all over the front and back pages of UK newspapers. The Swede's seriously active love life was of passing, yet voyeuristic, interest compared to his flirting between Chelsea and the national team. The Football Association was hoping – praying? – that they might go into the European Championships of 2004 with Eriksson's contract safely signed until 2008. But were there safecrackers in Soho Square trying to fiddle with that sacrosanct paperwork?

It was more a raffle than Raffles. You bought your ticket. Yet, one clue was that Sven-Goran Eriksson was more vocal than usual. He needed to be. 'What? Because of a cup of tea? I'm amazed every time this comes up because I have a contract. Yes, I will be England manager after the European Championship because I don't have an offer to go elsewhere, absolutely, and that's the truth.'

There was an element of general outrage – and, freezed in the frame like a bit of history, Eriksson hastily renewed his vows to England. It did not help Ranieri's situation or that of his team. Frank and the lads could sense the uncertainty and the effect it was having on all of them. And it was Ranieri's own success which led, arguably, to his failure to remain in west London.

Following up on their impressive win against Arsenal,

they had to play AS Monaco in the Champions League semi-final on 20 April 2004. There was a great deal of pressure. Ranieri would have preferred to be going up against Real Madrid. He was wary of Monaco. He was also upset by the news, whispered to him by one of football's Iagos, that Chelsea had been involved in meetings with people representing Jose Mourinho, then manager of FC Porto.

It made Ranieri much, much more determined to win. He changed, he tinkered mercilessly and he admits, 'That was my mistake.' He said the news of the Chelsea–Mourinho connection had influenced his judgement. He had made the wrong choices. The name of Jose Mourinho haunted him.

Chelsea lost 3–1 and did not recover in the second leg. They were out of the Champions League. Ranieri was asked whether if that had not happened he would have had a chance to drive Abramovich's car full-time, to be the new Schumacher. He just gave a huge shrug. And, indeed, who knows?

But you have to believe, along with Frank Lampard, that Jose Mourinho had been the long-time favourite for the high-performance driving seat. It just took a little time for someone to tell him. And how could he have imagined that, by the start of 2005, Chelsea's growing stature was such that three of England's most celebrated players, David Beckham, Steven Gerrard and Michael Owen, would possibly, and in a couple of cases probably, be wearing blue shirts by the summer of that year?

It's not just the money. The compliment to Mourinho is

that he knows how to pick and choose. Fantasy football? At Chelsea, they are playing it for real.

Frank – and the fans – could see nothing but glory. While never forgetting the heritage of the past, everything pointed to a 21st-century future. Frank had been taught that there is much to learn from tradition and Chelsea Football Club have plenty of that. And there was also the national team and Euro 2004. There was a lot to play for.

And that's always how Frank Lampard likes it.

Chapter Fourteen

New Beginnings

'In the end it was Frank once again who responded with
actions, letting his feet do the talking on the pitch.'

CLAUDIO RANIERI COMMENTING ON CHELSEA'S 1 MAY 2004 GAME AGAINST SOUTHAMPTON

Around the world, as the participants moved swiftly by
private jet and luxury yacht and shiny, polished
mahogany speedboats and other upmarket transport, the
machinations went on to replace Claudio Ranieri with Jose
Mourinho. It was never a question of if, simply when. For
Frank and the rest of the Chelsea team there were always
concerns. Yet, for Frank personally, the coaching of Ranieri
and the arrival of Abramovich had done nothing but good.
His profile was soaring. He was a first-team man of great
respect for Chelsea – and for England. It hadn't seemed a
moment ago that he'd have been happy to be in the squad,
even on the bench. Now, such thoughts were heresy.

The strategists at this point were Ranieri and Eriksson.
They had to get the ingredients right. Like perfumers, they
had to juggle the formula for their potions, to know the
exact combinations which, when brought together, would
provide winning results. If not, the team stank.

And, although Ranieri rotated his players at a dizzying rate, Frank was always in there. The Tinkerman's tinkering never helped cohesion but, whatever the game plan, Frank always played a significant part; he always retained the capacity to surprise. The schoolboy Jack-in-the-Box, the kid who would appear anywhere, did just that in his games of football. Most of the time.

Which is why there was much disappointment when he turned out for England for the friendly against Portugal on 18 February 2004. The 1–1 draw said a lot about the team, but there was also discussion about Frank not being sent in the right direction.

Much was written and much more said by the fans, but Paul Hayward in the *Daily Telegraph* got it spot on the day after the game: 'At Chelsea, Lampard is a puncher of holes, galloping from box to box to provide the team's midfield drive. At Stamford Bridge you will not find him in the team's Ryan Giggs position in front of the left back. He has neither the pace to get round the opposing right-back nor the natural inclination to distribute the ball with his left foot. It's not his fault.

'Lennox Lewis would give a horse a lousy ride in the Derby and Frankie Dettori would make a hopeless front-row forward. OK, so that is an exaggeration. It merely serves to illustrate the point that England will go into their opening match against France on 13 June with a deficiency Eriksson will somehow have to disguise.'

It was prescient about the competition in Portugal. It was also going to be quite a summer for Frank and Chelsea and England. Sven-Goran Eriksson is more sensitive than most in the football world and, some time before he announced the squad for Euro 2004, Frank knew that he would be playing a major role. There would be 'two teams' covering every position, but Frank and Beckham and Steven Gerrard were pivotal. As was – fingers crossed – Wayne Rooney, the goal cannon.

It was wonderful news. The pundits all kept saying that a style had to be developed to allow Frank to perform for England in exactly the way he was doing for Chelsea. What bigger praise? That the team had to accommodate his style – because it was that of a winner.

And Frank was on a run. Ranieri commented on his performance against Southampton on 1 May 2004: 'The outcome was decided in the space of eight minutes by goals from Frank Lampard – who else? I had read and heard about people saying that Frank's recent performances had not been as decisive as a few weeks before. These were foolish and inexpert comments. Frank Lampard had always been decisive for us, and, besides, could anyone be so blind as to miss the point that I had been asking him for a big physical effort, perhaps inordinately big, precisely because he was so fundamental to our cause.

'In the end it was Frank once again who had responded with actions, letting his feet do the talking on the pitch.'

Claudio Ranieri was fired as manager of Chelsea on the May Bank Holiday weekend in 2004. His final game in charge was against Leeds at the Bridge on 15 May 2004, and for most of the second half the fans chanted his name. It was a victory for Chelsea, 1–0.

It was also a victory for Ranieri and his strength of

character. As he said, he has a good character. As Ranieri's name echoed from the terraces, there was also a standing ovation for Frank and John Terry. Their outgoing manager paid tribute to them: 'They have been truly phenomenal this year but, best of all, they represent the real future of this team. A bright future, too, as there is nothing missing. The club has both money and the will to achieve.

'John Terry and Frank Lampard were already top players before working with me, as they had the right qualities within them. Perhaps I saw those qualities before they did and helped bring them out. I will always follow their progress and have a soft spot for them. They have become a part of me.'

Frank was with the England squad when Ranieri was sacked and he quickly got in touch with the former manager. He felt a strong bond with the man who had taken him over a bridge, from the traditions of West Ham to the glories of a continental Chelsea.

Football had changed since Frank's father's black-and-white television screened *Match of the Day*. And Claudio Ranieri was a kind introduction to the days of interactive, push-the-red-button plasma-technology soccer.

Understandably, it was a tense time for him. Here he was going into a major competition for his country, but what was happening to his role back at Chelsea? The commitment was all. Jose Mourinho pledged his allegiance. Sven-Goran Eriksson pledged his. All Frank Lampard had to do was play the game.

And for a very long time Frank Lampard was the star of England's debut in Euro 2004 at the Stadium of Light in

Lisbon. It was hot in Portugal – and so was Frank. Towards the end of the first half of their opening game against France, David Beckham clipped over a ball to Frank. He headed it powerfully, beating Fabien Barthez: England 1 France 0.

Crucially, there was no encore. France came back with eighty-eight minutes gone. The French captain, the captivating Zinedine Zidane, scored from a free-kick and a penalty. Stunned, Frank saw that glory eradicated, skilfully kicked away from under him.

For most of the match Frank Lampard had been England's greatest hero of the day. 'I have a very clear picture of that split second. It later sank in that, for a few minutes, I was a national hero. No one will even remember that I scored, now.'

Of course, they do. And Jose Mourinho, Frank's unknown admirer, had been there to see the goal.

After the 2–1 defeat against France, England beat Switzerland 3–0, Croatia 4–2 and then met Portugal in Portugal. It's easier to draw a shroud over it but – as in television programme *Friends* terms – its the one where Wayne Rooney limps off and England say goodbye to Euro 2004 losing 6–5 in penalties.

For Frank it had been an incredible summer: one that for him showed nothing but promise. It was clear that he was the number-one man for England and Chelsea, a club that was now one of the most talked about in the world.

There was interest in Beverly Hills, California, about the games – 'Is Frank playing?' – and he had emerged as a true Chelsea star, just like one of the legends of the past. The difference was that Chelsea were now a club that was being watched all over the world. Barking and Beijing? Who would have thought?

And at the same time another historical landmark was being established. Jose Mourinho, the engaging, brown-eyed handsome man, was the new boss. For Chelsea, football and Frank, it was a very, very new world to be living in. He'd watched his environment change – now what?

Chapter Fifteen
Moving the Goalposts

'It feels like a honour to train with them.'

FRANK LAMPARD, 18 NOVEMBER 2001

W est Ham had held such a personal attachment for Frank that it had been difficult to say goodbye. Yet, Chelsea had its own history. He made a point of learning about it: about how the club was formed in 1905 by the owners of the Stamford Bridge sports ground. Considering where the club was at now, we're talking science fiction. The 21st-century stadium forms part of Chelsea Village, a twelve-acre leisure and entertainment complex in SW6 which includes 291 four-star bedrooms, twenty-one conference and banqueting rooms, five themed restaurants and bars and the Chelsea Club and Spa.

The capacity of the stadium is 42,449, though the record attendance is the 82,905 supporters who turned up for the First Division derby against Arsenal on 12 October 1935. The cost of a season ticket for the Matthew Harding Upper Stand is £750, but you do get a nice meal.

The players' food is supervised by Chelsea's medical department who are responsible for choosing the menu, although the players are allowed to ask for a different meal according to their culture and habits. For Frank's East End memory, this was a whole new meaning of café society.

Frank went with Chelsea into their centenary year with ambitions of taking a unique haul of four trophies in one season: the Premier League, European Cup, FA Cup and Carling Cup. Not bad – especially when you consider their record.

Their one League title to date came in 1955, but that's helped by three FA Cup wins, two League Cups and two Cup-Winners' Cup wins. Chelsea now had the financial clout to go for it. The doom watchers were everywhere, the sniping constant. There was no arguing, however, with the money. In one of those lavish opinion polls for a strangely edited John Sweeney UK television documentary in February 2005 about Roman Abramovich's wealth, the reaction from fans was 'We don't care where the money comes from'. One fan put his face into the television camera and announced, 'We just want to WIN!' And the money, like the Russian oil, did not seem as though it would ever dry up.

Abramovich bought Chelsea in July 2003 for £59.3 million. The Russian had topped the 'Rich List' of the London newspaper the *Sunday Times* with a personal wealth of £7.5 billion, the highest in the UK, and, according to the influential American *Forbes* magazine's annual list of billionaires, the oil tycoon turned football fan is the world's 25th richest person.

Which is why his football club was creating some of the best training facilities in the world. They got the go-ahead to develop a £20 million training complex in Cobham, Surrey, by the end of 2004. The club moved into a temporary base on site and, when work is completed, facilities will include a moat, fifteen pitches, three of which will have undersoil heating, plus an indoor pitch covered by a dome, one of Europe's largest physiotherapy departments and a headquarters built partly underground.

If you study the architectural drawings, the steel-and-glass construction is instantly impressive. One design critic thought, 'For many years, Chelsea have trained on wind-blasted university pitches, on an unlovely patch of land between the M4 and a Heathrow runway.

'Now they are set to occupy a nerve centre more suitable to the Russian owner's vision of a consistently successful footballing force, sustained by their youth infrastructure, moving through domestic and European triumphs and eventually achieving global domination. They probably could not have chosen anywhere more suitable than Cobham. This is Premiership football in the 21st century.'

Which, naturally, is where Jose Mourinho came in. Or, rather, jumped out. When he was officially named as the man in charge at Chelsea, he announced, 'I'm not one who comes straight out of a bottle. I'm a special one.' And so he proved.

On his appointment, the new manager said he would not discuss individual players, but he did say, 'I love Lampard' – who was then the most improved footballer in the English game. It is no task to see the dynamic which links both Frank and his manager. They are both in it to win, for the glory and the cups.

They are fighters, competitors, people who come out of watching Russell Crowe in *Gladiator* and see it as a motivational movie. You take on all the competition – and you win. Mourinho had that to do from the off.

He had to dismantle the past. When he was publicly named as the new boss at Chelsea on 2 June 2004, he immediately launched into Claudio Ranieri. Naughtily, Ranieri had recently suggested it was a lot easier to win the championship in Portugal than it was in England.

Mourinho said, 'Mr Ranieri says it's easy to win in Portugal and I didn't like what I heard. I could say other things like: "He is in football for twenty years and the only thing he won in his career is the Spanish Cup." I could say that. I don't like to, but I could.'

Ranieri was clearly upset about what had gone on and he took it out on the man closest to him – the man taking his job. He mocked Mourinho's claim that he would win trophies in his first season; he boasted about meeting Spurs earlier that week but, of course, he had turned down the manager's job at White Hart Lane for Valencia. At the same time he was working out a 'package' with Chelsea.

The clever Mourinho took every opportunity to establish himself and he had the advantage of having won the Champions League with Porto only a week earlier – and of a £4.5-million-per-season, three-year contract at Chelsea. He was obviously indignant at Ranieri's suggestion that he could only win in Portugal: 'You should explain to him that if a team win the UEFA Cup or the

Champions League they have to play clubs from other countries.

'I didn't win the UEFA Cup and the Champions League playing twenty Portuguese teams. Tell him that to win the Champions League this year we beat Partizan Belgrade, Real Madrid, Marseilles, Manchester United, Lyon, Deportivo and Monaco.

It was after this Stamford Bridge encounter that Mourinho, Peter Kenyon and Roman Abramovich flew by the owner's private jet to Manchester. There, they met Chelsea's four England players – Frank, Wayne Bridge, John Terry and Joe Cole – at the national squad's hotel on the eve of Euro 2004. For Frank it was another endorsement of how much he mattered to the team – and to the team's future.

The first he knew of the meeting was a telephone call where he was simply told, 'He wants to see you.' They met for the first time in a private room at the hotel. Frank says his new boss stood in front of him, stared into his eyes and asked, 'Are you a winner?'

The sequence was replayed with his team-mates. 'It was a strange scene, but it felt right and walking out we all thought, We're going to win something this season. In a way, he asks us all that question every day. With him the only thing that matters is winning and that has rubbed off on everyone.'

At the same time the press wanted to stir things up and played Mourinho's comments from earlier that day to his predecessor at Chelsea. At the time, Ranieri was about to receive the Variety Club's Man of the Year award. He responded to Mourinho's remarks by suggesting that only the brave would boast about winning a trophy in his first season in England. 'We built a good foundation because I was wanting to finish my job. Mourinho showed a great performance with Porto, nothing more. Now he has to show this in England. It's different in England. Mourinho is the best coach. I could never say I'd win things in the first year.'

The self-deprecating Sir Bobby Robson, one of the most respected figures in football, could only back up Ranieri's assessment of Mourinho: 'No one knows Jose better than me. He was my interpreter at Sporting Lisbon and stayed with me every day for six years. I see some players leave their careers and get a manager's job in a week.

'He didn't do that. He then spent two years with Louis van Gaal at Barcelona, so in total he spent eight years with two quite decent managers. We had a very good working relationship and, once he'd found his feet, he was on the pitch with me every day. He was a good student and a great help to me, but I think he learned a lot, too. He was always very clever. He listened. He learned, he wrote down and remembered.

'When he first started I said, "Jose, stand there and tell me what the players, Luis Figo or anyone else, are muttering about me behind my back and, if you don't tell me every word, I'll get someone else."

'He knew what I was spelling out – I wanted total loyalty. I had to tell him how to be faithful to people. He quickly realised the importance of establishing a rapport with the players. He had never been a player at a high level, so he respected what they could do.

'Jose was a great guy with the players and they appreciated that. I gave him more and more responsibility as time went on and we developed a mutual respect. He is now a top-class coach.'

But the best in the world? Better than Arsène Wenger or Sir Alex Ferguson? Jose Mourinho believed it.

And Frank Lampard had no doubts. All that was required was the commitment in what would be some of the most exciting months of Frank's life and of his football club's history. All of which, according to Mourinho, was part of his destiny. He declared, 'I didn't want to be the best coach at forty and a has-been at fifty. I think I am the special one.'

If it all sounded like dialogue out of *Star Wars*, the fans were not complaining...

Chapter Sixteen

The Messiah

'I was ten years old and my father was sacked on Christmas Day. He was a manager. I know I will be sacked one day.'

JOSE MOURINHO, CHRISTMAS 2004

Frank took to Jose Mourinho just as he had taken to football, as his father said, 'like a duck to water'. From day one and why not? He was one of them.

As Frank continually pointed out, there was the manager's public face in the press conferences and the post-match television interviews, but with his players he was a different man. He was always a supporter. And he had total focus. In early 2005 he explained that one of the reasons he joined Chelsea was to help the club grow on and off the field. 'Peter Kenyon is completely focused on the Chelsea brand and making them one of the best clubs in the world. That makes me want to be part of the project.

'You can have top stars, the best stadium, the best facilities, the most beautiful project in terms of marketing, but if you don't win all the work is forgotten. You have to win.

'The new training centre will be fantastic; as is the way Mr Abramovich is ready to help the team in all the areas where you need big financial investment.

'But our role, mine and the players, in terms of achieving football success, becomes the nucleus of that. Mr Abramovich is not able to be here every day, but there was one thing I wanted him to know – he is always welcome.

'I always feel that with a president, or an owner: the players like to see him. When he comes here he is not coming to interfere with my work. He just comes to give us his faith, to give his support, to communicate with people. He's always present. He's committed. He knows what Mr Kenyon is doing, he knows what I am doing and he doesn't need to be worried about training players or the club organisation. Abramovich is a top man.

'I know how it works, though. I know football very well. I was nine or ten years old and my father was sacked on Christmas Day. He was a manager. The results had not been good. He lost a game on 23 December.

'On Christmas Day the telephone rang and he was sacked in the middle of our lunch. So I know all about the ups and downs of football. I know that one day I will be sacked. I know that one day the results will not be good...'

But not now Jose! He agrees he has no intention of 'the results will not be good' stuff coming anywhere true. Indeed, as Frank pointed out, he admits he is a Jekyll-and-Hyde character. 'Facing the press is easy, but you have to try to take positive things from these meetings. I try to have some messages I want to pass on. After a game against Liverpool I could guess how questions would go.

THE MESSIAH

Joe Cole scored the goal, Joe Cole goes to the national team, Joe Cole is not playing for Chelsea.

'I could guess they wanted to put Joe Cole on the moon. So, because he got all the plaudits from the press, I had to kick him a little bit. When I face the media I feel it is part of the game. I'm not there to be what they want me to be or say what people are waiting for me to say. It would be much easier if I could go and say, "Joe Cole was amazing and so on." But I need him to give me more. I don't go there to be part of the media movie. My movie is another one.'

Interestingly, Joe Cole, along with Frank, became one of the first of Chelsea's Euro 2004 stars to return to training, joining Mourinho's squad five days ahead of schedule. The new manager also made his mark on the world transfer market when, in July 2004, he made Didier Drogba the most expensive forward in the history of British football when Chelsea agreed to pay £23.2 million for the Marseilles goal-maker. A further £8 million invested in Benfica midfielder Tiago took the club's shopping bill to £31.2 million, more than a Ken Bates visit to Harrods and a record single-day spend for a Premiership club.

The financially dynamic duo were part of the investment which brought the record-breaking safe hands of Petr Cech and the tremendous skills of Arjen Robben, Paulo Ferreira and Mateja Kezman to Stamford Bridge. Not much short of £70 million, the total cost of Chelsea's six close-season arrivals equalled that spent on new recruits by the rest of the Premiership put together.

Drogba echoed the new era at Chelsea when he said, 'I wanted to stay at Marseilles because I have experienced

133

fantastic times there, but financially, and in a sporting sense, I could not refuse Chelsea's offer. I hope I live up to their expectations.

'I also had proposals from Italian clubs, but going to Chelsea is an interesting challenge in my career and I'm glad to join them. What convinced me to join Chelsea is that they really showed that they wanted me and that counts a lot. I will give my best for them now.'

For Mourinho it was a little like recruiting 'The Magnificent Seven'. He had to create a bunch of players that would conquer all.

An email in November 2004 from Paul Sweeney, a fan of thirty-seven years, told the players what he expected: 'I'd like to say that, just because we are lucky enough to be financially sound and have a squad able to challenge for the Premiership, this doesn't mean I want us to be part of any European Superleague.

'It is fantastic to play in the Champions League. However, speak to most Chelsea fans and the games they look out for are those involving old rivalries. We love playing Manchester United and Arsenal, but fixtures against Spurs, Leeds and West Ham etc. are just as big occasions.

'If Chelsea win the League for the first time since 1955, it will be a tremendous achievement and most of my Chelsea mates would take that over winning in Europe.

'Our new-found wealth has attracted a new breed of supporter, but there are still many thousands of us who care just as much now as we did when playing Shrewsbury on a wet Wednesday night. They'd agree with me in saying: stuff your European Superleague.'

I don't know if missives like that made Jose Mourinho reflective but, only a couple of weeks later, he said, 'The big question mark is, how long will it take to impose my ideas on the team? I'll never forget Mario Stanic. He left the club, but he was with me on the first day and said something like: "A lot of people have arrived in England and they adapt to the English reality of football. But I know that your methods and your philosophy and your way of thinking are very special. Don't ever change, even if it takes time, don't change."

'I'll never forget what he said. So it was a question for me whether the players could adapt. I followed an Italian manager and it cannot be easy when you follow a manager who thinks very differently.

'The pre-season became crucial for me. I analysed the way the players were open for the change. When you just work tactically, in pure football sessions, you can see the way the players think. I could see those like Frank who would become crucial to me because they thought the same way.

'Not just the players that I brought from Porto, who were a big help in that adaptation, but the other players like John Terry and Eidur Gudjohnsen.

'We play very good football. I have never had a match in five years where my team has had less possession than the opponents. Never, never. We could play Real Madrid, we could play Deportivo, even Manchester United, we always had a bigger percentage. At Chelsea, it will be the same.

'Fans are normally behind the team, faithful. They understand we are in good shape. But I always believe that on the day we will score the goals. If one day the result is 3–3 it doesn't change my mind, because football is football. It's normal. What is not normal is not scoring enough goals when you are playing good football.

'In England when people go to football they just think about football. Nothing else. They enjoy every second, so the atmosphere is fantastic, and it takes the pressure off you because you also become involved in that spirit. The best place to work in football is England.

'In my early days I was in love with Liverpool, with Keegan, Dalglish and Souness. But Chelsea jumped in front of everyone because they were open and direct; they came direct to me and I have no doubts in my mind that I made the right decision.

'My heart told me to come to England, not to Italy or Spain. If my future can be in England and Chelsea I would love that. But I have to keep winning matches.

'Maybe I was lucky to find a team with a Lampard and a Terry in it – they represent the mental approach to the game in England. I believe I can do good things in England.'

But he knows there are no guarantees, no security of tenure. 'I remember Sir Bobby Robson and the first time he was sacked. He was sixty-four years old, at Sporting Lisbon and they were top of the league, so you never know…

'When it arrives I won't cry. I will enjoy my family and then, the next week or maybe in a month, I'll get another club. Remember, the richest managers are those who are sacked the most.'

An intriguing contrast – one that bridges the worlds of both Frank Lampards, and Jose Mourinho and Tommy

Doherty, Chelsea Football Club managers – are the memories of Roy Bentley, who celebrated his eightieth birthday in 2005. He was part of the England team that was caught wrong-footed by the United States in the 1950 World Cup – America's goalkeeper that day was an undertaker and they did bury England – and centre-forward and captain of Chelsea's League Championship-winning team of 1955.

'When I look at Jose Mourinho's team I can see the maximum utilisation by each player of his particular talents.'

But where was this miracle from? Long before Jose Mourinho achieved success as a coach he thought of being a great player like his father, Felix Mourinho. The elder Mourinho had kept goal for Vitoria Setubal, Belenenses and Portugal and, as his only son, Jose was brought up to believe that he, too, had footballing genius within him.

But, although Jose – 'Ze' to his team-mates – had great motivational ability, he was not a great defender. At nineteen, Ze could not command a first-team place with Rio Ave, the unfashionable First Division side that Felix was managing. A yellowing newspaper report of what happened then recounts: 'In 1982 came his chance. While warming up against Sporting Lisbon, Rio Ave's first-choice goalkeeper was injured and Felix summoned his son to the dressing room to get changed.

'Embarrassingly, he never made it on to the pitch. When Rio Ave's then president, Jose Maria Pinho, learned that Ze was about to wear Ave's green-and-white striped jersey he issued an ultimatum: either Felix rescinded his decision or both he and his son were fired.

'Mourinho had to watch the match from the stands from where he saw his father's team lose 7–1.'

That was the point, it is said, when Mourinho decided that he would never be humiliated again and set his sights on becoming a top coach, even going so far as to expunge 'professional footballer' from his CV. The story also explains his methodical, unemotional approach to dealing with players and the almost perverse pleasure he seems to take in confronting management.

But, as the world looked on, it seemed as though there was nothing but big, blue skies for Jose Mourinho in August 2004. Any dark clouds were way back in the past. From then on, the guessing game was over whether Chelsea were going to win the Premiership. There were other trophies on offer, but this was about being better than Arsenal and Manchester United, about being England's number one. It was what all the investment was about. It was about establishing a worldwide brand. It was what winning was about.

Chapter Seventeen

The Rivals

'He leaves absolutely nothing to chance.'
FRANK LAMPARD ON JOSE MOURINHO, 11 DECEMBER 2004

'It was up to me to convince my players that Alex Ferguson's problem was that he was scared of us.' That is Jose Mourinho recalling a time when he was with Porto and his club were up against Manchester United in the Champions League. He explained further: 'At the time he was a top manager; he smelled and felt he could beat us.' He couldn't. And the rivalry, friendly but edgy, continued in England when Chelsea leapfrogged up the table. Yet the English Premiership of 2004–05 was so, so different from the Champions League. Even before Christmas 2004, Mourinho said, 'We have attitude and it will be difficult to catch us.'

The United manager and his players were very aware of that but, as George Best pointed out in February 2005, when you have to rely on another team to lose, the game is usually already up.

Frank and the team were superbly pumped up for the 15 August 2004 game against United, their first major encounter and test for the new boss. Before every match a player is chosen by Mourinho to make a motivational speech. Frank explained, 'It's about bonding and it's a way of bringing out people's characters. We stand in the dressing room, put our arms around each other and one of us says a few words and finishes by asking, "Who are we?!" Everyone shouts, "We are CHELSEA!!!"

'There are a few lads, like Damien Duff, who are a bit quiet and it's a way of bringing them out of themselves as well as getting everyone motivated. Scott Parker did the best one at Newcastle. It was the most aggressive speech I'd ever heard – about being ready for battle.

'We already had a good spirit, but the manager has taken it a step further. There's a real belief in all of us that Chelsea is the place to be.

'The manager will have a joke, but the only thing that matters is winning. There is never a moment when you are allowed to relax. There's nothing that happens in a game that we haven't spoken about.

'He tells us we'll start in a particular way, but that if the game pans out differently then we will change and play this way. Everything is explained in such detail that the minute he does make a change we can adjust.

'We are able to do it because he leaves absolutely nothing to chance; he even tells us how to play if we go a goal up or down.

'He knows every opponent inside out. Even their subs. He talks to us as a team, but also individually. No player likes to be blanked by the manager, because even if you're playing well you still wonder what he's thinking.

'Before there wasn't quite the belief that there is now.'

That conviction was evident in Mourinho's first game with Chelsea against the man who would become his nemesis, Sir Alex Ferguson. They played lots of mind games, with both seeking the psychological advantage. They had a mental history together. After Porto's 2–1 win over Manchester United in the Champions League last-sixteen first leg in Portugal, Ferguson accused Mourinho's players of being from Central Casting, actors, divers. Well, it was a little more grown up than alleging they'd wasted more balls than Marilyn Monroe.

Mourinho, showing that he was equally capable of playing with an opponent's mind, observed that the Scottish manager had been 'a bit emotional' and was clearly upset to see his side 'dominated by a club with only 10 per cent of his budget'.

Contradicting the reporting at the time, Mourinho says Ferguson never refused to shake his hand at the end of the game and that, when Porto won in the second leg at Old Trafford, he came to the dressing room to congratulate him. 'He felt he could maybe put some pressure on us,' Mourinho has said of Ferguson's pre-match remarks. 'I understood it. I work my players and I work the press conference to try to put a good atmosphere around my team. We play, we won, finish, shake hands. That's it.

'I have no problems with him [Ferguson]. He complained about certain things in Porto, but he shook my hand after the match, and at Old Trafford he came to the dressing room to do it.

'I have respect for every manager when they have respect for me.'

Time moved on and the two men stand on different pedestals. Both are huge winners. Mourinho has so quickly become his own myth. 'Self-esteem bigger than the Sagrada Familia cathedral,' said one Spanish newspaper. They also describe him as *chuto*, which translates as swaggering or swanky. But, indeed, *chuto* enough in March 2005 to be getting paid £750,000 by American Express to endorse the buying power and benefits of that particular organisation.

European footballing deity Johan Cruyff was asked how the Portuguese man of war would sail in new waters at Chelsea. 'In terms of trophies, you can't say a word against him after he won everything in Portugal and Europe. But Mourinho needs to be more attacking than he was at Porto. And mastering attacking football is the hardest thing in the game.'

But would the Russian billions put a prevailing wind in his sails? Without getting too mathematical, the 'New' Chelsea had spent more on players in one year than Ferguson had done in more than eighteen years at Old Trafford.

The game at Stamford Bridge on 15 August 2004 was much about who was going to run English football's Camelot. Mourinho was questioned before the game and was wonderful: 'I hope we have many, many rounds because if you have many rounds it means Sir Alex still feels young and stays at Manchester United and it means that my work is going well and I stay here for many seasons. I hope we have ten rounds, fifteen rounds – just until the final whistle...'

Later, he went on, 'I'm a European champion and I think I'm a special one. If I wanted an easy job, I would have stayed at Porto – beautiful blue chair, the Champions League trophy, God, and, after God, me.

'I'm not here to be a bighead, to claim responsibility for all the good things. I'm here to co-operate with others, to try to make this club better and to help the players become better.'

Mourinho walks the positive-thinking tightrope between confidence, arrogance and superego. But the belief, be it from motivational manuals or the experience of years, is relentless. He was certain Chelsea could win the Premiership in his first season in charge: 'One hundred per cent. I have no doubts that we can.'

The always likeable Claudio Ranieri had won nothing of real consequence in nearly two decades in management, while Mourinho had won the UEFA Cup, Portugal's League and Cup Double and the European Cup in two superb seasons at Porto. A decade or more ago, when Ferguson was winning the Premier League with United, Mourinho taught physical education in Lisbon. After helping out with the scouting and coaching on an ad hoc basis at a variety of small professional clubs, he was appointed by Sporting Lisbon as an interpreter for the incoming manager, Bobby Robson.

Robson was sufficiently impressed to take his protégé

with him to Porto and then to Barcelona, by which stage he had been promoted to assistant coach. Then, in 1997, Robson made way for Louis van Gaal and Mourinho was the only member of Sir Bobby's staff who stayed with the Dutchman. 'I did it because I knew the club and the players. I wanted to go with Bobby when he left for PSV Eindhoven in 1998, but he urged me, as a friend, to stay at Barcelona because he said I would learn a lot.'

He took the advice and continued his education under van Gaal, working with Rivaldo, Figo and Patrick Kluivert. When the Dutch coach went, Barca asked him to assist the replacement, Lorenzo Serra Ferrer. By now, however, he had decided that it was time to go it alone. Benfica offered him his first job as head coach, but Portugal's most celebrated club was hamstrung by financial problems and a power struggle in the boardroom. Mourinho resigned after three months.

It was with unfashionable Uniao de Leiria that he started to make a name for himself, guiding them to fifth place in the League – their highest-ever finish.

When Porto came calling, he said on taking charge that the team he had inherited was the club's worst for twenty-six years and added, 'But next season we will be champions.'

And they were. To the amazement of the fans, he was as good as his word, adding the UEFA Cup for good measure; Celtic were his victims in the final.

'One of the characteristics of that side was that they weren't afraid to lose and a team that isn't afraid is going to play better and win more often. When we did lose, we were cheered because we had fought well.'

THE RIVALS

In his second season, they fought well enough to dispatch all-comers in the Champions League. Manchester United went in March 2004, beaten 2–1 in Portugal, then held 1–1 at Old Trafford in two matches still memorable for Ferguson's complaints about gamesmanship.

Chelsea's inspirational leader remembers the two games very well indeed. 'We saw it as a chance to prove to ourselves that we could beat a bigger team who, apparently, had more potential than us. I tried to transmit the confidence I had to the players.

'It was the opening of our new stadium the night we played United, so I told my team to enjoy the atmosphere and enjoy the game. I told them to go out and compete with United, and to get the feel of whether they could beat them or not. After a while, they knew they could.

'At that particular time our best strikers were injured and unavailable, so we had to play a different system. Our plan was to control the play and have a big percentage of possession. We didn't have enough attacking potential to go and play the game in their half, so the key was the quality of our passing.

'Portuguese football has good qualities and bad ones. One of the good ones is the ability the players have to play the possession game. In the matches against Manchester United, this allowed us to control the play.'

And here they were again, facing off. Mourinho had no problems with that. 'There is no comparison between a League match and a knock-out competition. Also, my players at Chelsea are completely different from the ones I had at Porto, and the way we play here at the moment is different. Manchester United will also be different.

'When we played them last season, it was at a time when they weren't feeling good. They weren't playing well. This season we have them in the opening game, and at the start everybody feels good and ready. For these reasons, in preparing for this match, I didn't give a single thought to Porto–United.

'We have to be more direct, because the opposition approach things differently. In Portugal we played a game based on position and possession. The opposition didn't push up and pressurise us, they stayed back and let us play. English football is entirely different, so the Chelsea I'm building will be a mixture of what I like in my teams and what I think is possible.'

Mourinho was not fazed by the financial clout he had over United and Arsenal. It was more matter-of-fact: 'It's true that, when we go after a player, we are normally in a position to get him. But there is another difference between us. Their managers have been in place for many years and I've been here for one month. It's a big advantage that they know everything about their players. And I mean everything.

'Maybe they know certain players better than they know some members of their own family, because they've been with them every day for years.

'I was at Porto for just two years and I knew everything about those players, so I can imagine it's fantastic when you work with basically the same group for many years.

'Then you can work on new things, because the ideas you had to teach them first have become established and automatic. New players will have to learn the unique requirements of English football before they can operate at optimum efficiency.

'At the same time, those who were already here need to learn from me what I want. My mind is always open to new ideas. That way, every day I should be better than I was the day before. I'll still be saying the same when I'm sixty.'

With his arrival and the team around him, Mourinho was confident that they could compete successfully in all competitions. After waiting fifty years, the fans would love them to win the Premiership, but Mourinho's personal preference would be to get his hands on the European Cup again. Or would it be again?

'I won it, but I never touched the cup. I kissed it when it was there, next to the UEFA president, but then I got my medal and walked away. I want to win it again, because I don't even have a photo with the cup.

'I had no time for that. The cup went to the captain and then the players. After that there was the team photo. My kids were there with my wife, and I went to see them, then I went to the press conference.

'After that I went home, and the next day I flew to Monaco to meet Mr Abramovich and Peter Kenyon, so I didn't participate in the celebrations.'

Kenyon, now a controller at Stamford Bridge, was naturally very familiar with Ferguson at Old Trafford and was enthusiastic that Mourinho could work the same magic at Stamford Bridge. In turn, Mourinho wants to create his own dynasty, his own reputation. 'I don't want to be compared with other people. I am what I am, I've done what I've done, and I will try to do well again in the future.

'But I know that one day, instead of being a champion at the end of the season, I'll get the sack. These things happen in football. I don't think I'm the best in the world when I win, and I don't think I'm the worst when I lose. I'm just me.'

And the head-to-head against United? 'If we win, we are not champions and, if we lose, we are not out of the fight. It is just one match, no more important than any other.'

That's not how many other people saw it. Especially Frank and the team. And an old friend of Frank's boss. 'Jose showed by confronting Alex at Porto last season that he won't hide or let anyone undermine him,' said Sir Bobby Robson, adding, 'He won't ever be vulgar, but he will challenge Alex or Arsène if he thinks they are wrong.'

Most people were already certain of that. And there was word that Mourinho was the equal of Alex Ferguson and his infamous 'hairdryer' rages. Mourinho was asked about his temper when he got the Chelsea job. 'It's possible at half-time I will throw teacups.

'Temper? I kicked a garbage can at Victor Baia once. It was half-time and I didn't expect to hit him. I can understand what happened with Fergie, the boot and David Beckham…

'But I don't want players to be afraid of me and I never want to appear aloof or faraway. I want them to feel they can be open with me. You need the feedback for them to develop the best way.

THE RIVALS

'The best way for the players to believe in what they are doing is for the players to participate. The days of managers arriving and pointing at things on a blackboard are finished.'

Chapter Eighteen
Who is That Man?

'To score against Chelsea would be great. I like Mourinho. I watch their games on the telly and can't wait to hear him speak afterwards. He's so honest and he just wants to win.'

SPURS STRIKER JERMAIN DEFOE, 15 JANUARY 2005

Jose Mario Santos Mourinho Felix was born in Seteubal, Portugal, on 23 January 1963. After that, it's all theory. He's tried to prevent people writing about his non-football life and his family from talking about him. It doesn't seem as though the intention is to protect his privacy – it's more to do with conundrum-creating, shrouding the personal details to deepen the mystery.

This puzzle of a man certainly does not want his opponents to know what he's thinking; even Frank and the other players are never quite sure if he's giving them the whole plan. There's often a need-to-know atmosphere in the dressing room. It's all part of the grand tactical plan.

Sam Allardyce was the manager of Bolton at the beginning of 2005 and had been suggested as a possibility to replace Sven-Goran Eriksson as the England coach. He's a roustabout sort of person and is as entranced as everyone else about Mourinho.

What makes him tick? Allardyce made some valid points, 'I am on the LMA (League Managers' Association) committee and the figures they produce on managers are staggering. Out of the 450 managers who have managed in the past four years, only fifty are still managing. So to stay in the game as a manager for over ten years is an achievement.

'Mourinho intrigues me. What fascinates me is that he has built this great career when he was never really a footballer himself. That's the hard route. He's had to convince everybody he could do this job because there was no track record as a player. What was he? Interpreter for Bobby Robson? Abramovich has given him the means to have the best players, but he must mould them into a team and he seems to be achieving that almost immediately. That's not down to his coaching, that's his man-management.

'He has a hard exterior, but I don't believe that's what he's about. There is a compassionate side, a side that shows a lot of humility, and that is why he is as good as he is. In public I know he can come across as arrogant, but I don't see him as that. John McGrath, my old coach at Preston, used to say, "The arrogant man doesn't learn because he thinks he knows it all."'

The Bolton manager went on to say that many people at Porto despised him for leaving halfway through his two-year contract. He said Mourinho was ruthless enough to break the contract to pursue a greater challenge and

Above: Michael Owen salutes Frank's vital goal for England against France.

Below: A multi-million-pound line up: Wayne Rooney watches Frank and Rio Ferdinand enjoy another victorious England moment.

He's on the superstar money and part of it comes from lucrative sponsorship deals, including his ongoing arrangement with adidas.

The contender. He was runner-up to Thierry Henry for the PFA Player of the Year Award in 2004 and narrowly missed the honour in April 2005 when his great friend, Chelsea captain John Terry, picked up the trophy.

Above: On the ball: which foot will it be? He scores with them both and The Shed are happy either way …

Below: Frank fan Sven-Goran Eriksson presents his regular player with the FA's England Player of the Year Award.

Above left: A moment of changing-room chic and a rare photograph – Frank on the bench.

Above right: London Knightsbridge resident Frank on the town with Spanish girlfriend Elen Rives.

Below: Giving something back: a dedicated supporter of the Teenage Cancer Trust, Frank also encourages youngsters in sport: here he is feeding schoolchildren's appetites in London's Battersea.

Medals all round: with a happy, smiling Jose Mourinho behind them, Chelsea's English duo of Frank and John Terry celebrate their Carling Cup triumph.

Above: Seen here with John Terry, Roman Abramovich and Eidur Gudjohnsen, Frank celebrates winning the Premiership at Stamford Bridge in May 2005. The Blues' fifty-year wait had come to an end.

© *John Ingledew*

Below: In December 2005, Lampard came second behind Ronaldinho of Brazil in the glittering FIFA World Player of the Year awards in Zurich. Samuel Eto'o of Cameroon was third.

Frank, a devoted family man, with his wife and their baby, Luna, out and about in town.

Allardyce understood that. 'If Chelsea had come to me, I would have said yes. No question. You are talking about its backer creating a monster that might not be caught for the next decade. If the manager gets it right.'

So who is the man in charge of the future of Chelsea and Frank? The man asked to change money into trophies? Frank said, 'He does get very angry when he loses. The manager is a winner, he only wants to win, and that's the attitude needed at Chelsea. We are all from him. We have become more attacking but our team talks haven't changed. Mourhino still says, "Go out and win the game." He doesn't care whether it's by 1–0 or 4–0.'

Mourinho gave one wonderful quote shortly after his appointment but, as often with the more outrageous ones, there was a twinkle in the brown eyes: 'I don't have to control Mr Abramovich. He has to control me.'

It is clear it was the challenge which made him leave the comfort of his blue chair and God-like status at Porto. Some argue that having won the Champions League at the age of forty-one Mourinho had achieved all that he could at Porto. He arrived at Chelsea with outward humility. 'Obviously, if I don't reach my goals perhaps I will have to go home. But I don't think this will happen. I think at the end of my contract Chelsea will be interested in giving me a new one.'

A host of views followed and, amalgamated with interviews and of those around him, this is a profile of the man holding Frank's and Chelsea's fortunes in his hands. Frank has no doubts. But this is the man: Mourinho is deep into UEFA training manuals and fitness theory (he holds several physical education qualifications), and he is obsessed with detail and preparation. We know his rules.

From the moment his Chelsea players get up to the moment they go to sleep, every minute of their day is programmed by Mourinho and his assistants from Portugal, Rui Faria and Andre Villas Boas.

It was the end of the long nights at China White and a new regimen of early-morning alerts and ninety-minute training sessions. 'From here each practice, each game, each minute of your social life must centre on the aim of being champions,' Mourinho wrote to his Chelsea squad in early July 2004.

'First-teamer will not be a correct word. I need all of you. You need each other. We are a TEAM.'

To make absolutely clear what he was saying at the end of the letter, Mourinho offered the equation: 'Motivation + Ambition + Team + Spirit = SUCCESS.'

It was a replica of the letter he sent to Porto players when he was appointed their manager in January 2002. Mourinho handed the Code of Conduct charter to every Chelsea player when they arrived for pre-season training on 5 July 2004.

Frank said the message was clear: any wrongdoing and the player was out. Mourinho explained his point: 'I presented the players with a document containing the rules they have to live by at this club. And anyone who breaks them will be out. I'm not saying they can't go out and have a drink, but they need to be able to train at the highest level. If a player goes to bed at three in the morning, it's obvious he won't be able to train at peak the next day.'

WHO IS THAT MAN?

Chelsea, which from the swinging sixties had been a party club, felt the Continental draught. The Jose Mourinho rules, like those imposed at Porto, stated, 'Any player caught out late the night before training will be out the door. Players arriving late for training will be fined and given a final warning. Every team member must follow medical advice given to them. Players will only speak English while on team duty. No cliques between race or nationality factions are allowed.'

Mourinho was adamant: 'I won't necessarily need twenty-four spies to follow all my players around because it will be obvious to me which ones have broken the rules by the way they train and play.

'I know it's hard for a young player these days to stay out of trouble off the pitch because of the people that sometimes gather around them and the money they have, but I expect all my players to behave. If an injured player does not turn up for his medical treatment then he is not desperate to come back and isn't worried about winning the title. I'm not telling them they can't drink. I am simply telling them when and how.

'If a player does not have a match until the following Saturday, then it's OK for him to drink after the game with his friends or family. But not if he has a game during the week.

'It's vital to build the team around winners. If I want a player and he talks money for half an hour and doesn't ask about facilities or ambition, then I don't want him. And I don't like having eleven nationalities in a side. I want players to adapt to the English mentality.

'They have to speak English when we are in a group. There will be no cliques here with the French sitting in one corner and the black players sitting in another, for instance.

'If I speak to Claude Makelele privately I will talk to him in French, but in a group I will speak to them in English. If they don't know the language, they will have to study.'

Significantly, when Mourinho arrived at Porto they were not doing well in Portugal's First Division. The following year they won the treble of domestic league and cup and UEFA Cup. In 2003 Mourinho made history, becoming the youngest manager to lift the Champions League trophy.

Mourinho says he knew as a teenager that he would never become a first-class player. And, if he couldn't be first class, what was the point?

He began to learn everything he could about coaching, which is why at nineteen and at Rio Ave, he was already studying physical education. 'When you have a father, ex-top player, and your dream is to be like him but you feel you couldn't do it, your motivation comes from that point. I want to be really big in football. I feel I have some conditions to be a coach and manager. I start doing it. I start loving it. I go to university and study sports science. This is a real passion and methodology.'

Football's George Clooney – a man who at some games actually produces a viewable and entertaining *Ocean's Eleven* – with his expensively groomed hair, stubble and tan (fading in west London), leaves his enviable Eaton

Square apartment for Chelsea's training ground each morning at 7am.

This *Upstairs, Downstairs* environment is not a long way from his beginnings, if we consider his aunt, Maria Jose Ulke. His father Felix was the son of a ship's cook, but Mourinho's mother, Maria Julia, was from, if not exactly Portuguese aristocracy, then the nearest thing that Setubal, the town south of Lisbon where Mourinho grew up, had to a ruling class. Taken in as a child by her uncle, Mario Ledo, a sardine cannery boss who grew rich under the far-right regime of dictator Antonio de Oliveira Salazar, Maria Julia grew up in a mansion surrounded by servants and political intrigue. As well as presiding over the cannery union, Mario Ledo had built the Vitoria Setubal football stadium, and Ulke says that from an early age Maria Julia impressed on her son that she expected similarly great things from him.

When, after his death, Ledo's assets were seized in Portugal's bloodless 1974 coup, the family had to downgrade, but Maria Julia and Felix were allowed to keep Ledo's rambling mansion in Aires, complete with an elderly retainer against whom the young Mourinho practised his defending skills.

An authoritative European account reported, 'Mourinho refuses to talk about this period. Nor will he discuss his mother's influence, except to say, "I think I was always competitive. I don't trace it to one side of my family."'

In March 2005, when Frank had become more and more of Mourinho's family, the psychologist Oliver James, author of among other books *They F*** you up: How To*

Survive Family Life, was asked to make an assessment of the Chelsea manager.

'On a superficial reading the best person to compare him with is Brian Clough – but there are huge differences.

'Clough's moods swung violently, he drank, and was essentially unhappy. I don't sense that with Mourhino.

'There is a playfulness to him which is more important than the narcissistic desire to show off or the desire to impose himself on everyone else, which one gets a very strong sense of with Ferguson.

'Both Ferguson and Arsène Wenger have a strong sense of unfulfilled ambition, but with Mourhinho there is a joy to what he does, which is more than a desire to crush the opposition.

'He does not need to shit on everyone else to make himself feel better. He is unusual in being a famous, very good-looking man and not only is he faithful but uxorious. He has said a couple of times that his family is more important than football and he does this to encourage people to see that he has things in proportion.

'Very importantly, I think he is not primarily motivated by the achievement of the goal but by the process of winning. The satisfaction he gains from his working life is persuading the players to play to the best of their abilities and getting them to play in the right way rather than a frantic need for glittering prizes. He has a flexibility to his thinking which is very rare.'

Which is what Frank Lampard had always responded to. There were always instructions about doing the correct job, being in the perfect role, being a star. By doing that, Oliver James's glittering prizes became a right rather than a challenge.

Joel Neto, a Portuguese journalist discovered that when, at twenty-three, it was clear Jose Mourinho wouldn't go any further as a footballer, his mother signed him up for business school. He attended for just one day, before quitting the very next to enrol at Lisbon's Instituto Superior de Educacao Fisica (Isef).

'I believe that was the most significant day of his life,' says Neto. 'The day he said to himself, "I'm going to prove to my mother that I can make a living from football."'

Mourinho seldom speaks about his family. According to Neto, he never mentions Ledo or his own political views and, soon after Porto won the UEFA Cup, Neto learned that he visited his mother's house and removed all the family photographs from the walls to ensure they would never be published.

Neto further alleges that for years Mourinho sought to keep his footballing past secret. Indeed, Bobby Robson apparently only learned about Mourinho's Rio Ave career when he and Mourinho were invited to dinner by Pinho, the former club owner. Neto argues that Mourinho's attempt to control the past also extends to the present.

He knows everything about his players – what time they go to bed, what they eat, how long they train. Mourinho wants to control every aspect of their lives.

As an example of Mourinho's zeal, Neto cites his 'bible'

– Mourinho's name for the training manual, updated daily, containing his unexpurgated thoughts and reflections on football. According to Neto, Mourinho began compiling the bible in the early 1990s when he was employed as a fitness trainer at Estrela Amadora. But the event that brought the work into focus was the sudden death of his sister, Teresa, in 1996. The cause of Teresa's death is uncertain. Mourinho was devoted to her (although they had different interests growing up, he used to accompany her to horse riding and swimming lessons) and there is no doubt the loss affected him deeply.

Of his sister's death he said, 'It was a dark moment for our family.'

The following month his wife, Tami, gave birth to their first child, Matilde (Jose followed four years later) and learned that Bobby Robson had been offered the Barcelona job and that he would be moving to Spain with him. 'So on one side the bad things of life, next thing, the good things in life.'

Mourinho accepts that family is at the centre of his life and that he brings the same kind of commitment to football. It is a commitment he expects his players to share. At the 2004 pre-season briefings he warned his squad, 'Don't tell me one week later that you don't like the weather, or the family is not happy in England. I don't want a player who is not totally committed to my methodology.'

It has been said that Mourinho prefers bullish, nononsense players with old-fashioned virtues, but he insists it's not true. According to Mourinho, he and Tami used to have a German shepherd, 'Gullit' named after Ruud Gullit. For Mourinho, Gullit was 'an unbelievable player... an attacking, creative player but, at the same time, with fitness, power and mental strength'.

Gullit, we know, also a manager of Chelsea, understands the Mourinho thinking. 'A determination to win; you see it in the eyes of the players,' was how he saw it.

Mourinho agrees: 'That's my philosophy, too. Motivation is the most important thing. Some of them can and they don't want, some of them want and they can't. We want players who can do it and at the same time want to do it.

'When you look now at Chelsea players' CVs, they are similar to those of Porto's players before I arrived. Nobody won important things. You have two European champions here, Claude Makelele and Paulo Ferreira. But nobody won the Premiership. No one has the taste of big victories.'

Frank gave his view in the spring of 2005. 'He works with you, not only as a player but also as a personality. You can see it, not just in me but in Joe Cole and John Terry too.

'He has improved our ability to play in formation and adapt to different styles. It is obvious from the moment you meet the man that he has belief in himself and you can't help but let that rub off on you.

'The change in 2005 has been a change to a winning mentality; a belief that not only the manager has but the whole staff around him.'

Who is this guy? He's the one who insists that coming second – not winning – is no longer a consideration at Chelsea. When he arrived at Stamford Bridge, the new manager asked each of his players to his office for a chat. The boss recalled, 'I told Adrian Mutu, you are already a rich boy, you won a lot of money, you are still in a big contract. So no problem with your future about money, no problem about prestige in your home country. When you go back to Romania you will be one of the kings. But five years after you leave football nobody remembers you. Only if you do big things. This is what makes history.'

He also has a sense of humour. He wasn't much of a player and neither was Sven-Goran Eriksson or Arsène Wenger. But why did they succeed in management? 'More time to study,' deadpans Mourinho.

After graduating from Isef, Mourinho coached the youth team at Vitoria Setubal and attended courses under Andy Roxburgh at the Scottish Football Association. According to Faria, now Chelsea's fitness trainer, one of the first tricks Mourinho learned was the importance of having players face away from the sun when he addressed them so they should not be blinded (maybe it was so he could see the Glasgow kiss coming).

Next came the assistant trainer's position at Estrela Amadora, followed, in 1992, by his big break as assistant to Sir Bobby Robson at Sporting Lisbon. Although Mourinho was appointed as much for his translating as for his coaching skills (besides Portuguese and English, he speaks Spanish, Italian and some German), he had soon made himself invaluable, providing Sir Bobby with a superb analysis of his club's rivals.

Together, Robson and Mourinho won two Portuguese league titles, followed, in their first season in Spain, by the

European Cup-Winners' Cup. Mourinho acknowledges that it was from Robson that he got 'the idea of what it is to be a top coach'.

According to Roxburgh, the other key influence was Robson's successor at Barcelona, the Dutchman Louis van Gaal. 'Bobby and Louis were his real finishing school,' explained Roxburgh adding, 'His real education came on the front line.'

Roxburgh maintains that in the upcoming years Mourinho has overtaken both of them with his zeal and attention to detail. Evidence? Look at the final of the UEFA Cup in Seville in 2003, which Porto eventually won 3–2.

Later, Roxburgh welcomed Mourinho to UEFA's elite coaches forum. 'Jose told me he actually prepared his team to play for the silver goal,' said Roxburgh adding, 'In other words, how they would play – and this is exactly what happened against Celtic – to retain the ball for that first fifteen-minute period. That's what I call good coaching.'

In order to reach Seville, Porto first had to overcome Lazio in the semi-final second-leg in Rome. There was just one problem: although Porto led 4–1 from the first leg, Mourinho had been banned from the bench for the return game for earlier touchline misdemeanours.

A solution? He brought text-messaging to football. He dictated his instructions from the stands. There were thirty texts in all. Boas, who had to take Mourinho's ideas and transmit them to the bench said, 'Usually, he gives many more messages, but he had to be careful because if he had been caught he would have been in trouble. Jose prefers to be on the bench so that he can have direct contact with the team. He wants everything – the training sessions, the match reports and the game itself – to be controlled.'

We all know what a volatile game football is and how emotions can run riot. Mourinho suffered this at the sharpest end of all. After the Champions League final in Gelsenkirchen in May 2004, when Porto had beaten Monaco 3–0, Mourinho, who had respectfully collected his winner's medal, made straight for the players' tunnel. There had been death threats against his family, but he also felt like a leper, someone who was going.

He commented in his book *Mourinho*, published in Portugal and the UK in 2004, 'Sometimes the pressure reached a level worthy of a Don Corleone.'

Outside that, he said of his Porto detractors, 'Before the match people inside the club knew it was going to be my last game and they changed their behaviour towards me. This was from people who were next to me for two-and-a-half years, people who should think, This guy gave us a lot and we are in this final because of him, and should accept my desire to leave the club and go on to a new life.'

Much of the atmosphere is believed to have been because of upset Porto fans and agents. Why should their saviour be allowed to go somewhere else? There were lots of sticks and stones. He was accused of having a love affair.

In fact, they accused him of everything except being able to turn a football team into winners. In turn, he believed Porto had no complaints about his conduct in joining Chelsea.

An investigation by one British newspaper gave some of

the background to that drama. 'Peter Kenyon began courting Mourinho soon after Porto's draw at Old Trafford took them to victory in the last sixteen – a dramatic, last-minute success that, at the end of the game and in contrast to his behaviour in Gelsenkirchen, saw Mourinho dashing along the touchline with uncontained glee. But Mourinho says he refused to meet Abramovich until after the final whistle in Germany: that would have been unseemly while Chelsea and Porto were potentially still in competition with one another. "I told them I didn't want bad things appearing in the press."

'Instead, and this is also characteristic of Mourinho and his working methods, he sent Abramovich a Powerpoint presentation with a detailed breakdown of Chelsea's squad, his assessment of which players should stay and who should go, and what he expected from the club in terms of training, scouting and medical facilities. When Mourinho finally met Abramovich on his yacht in Monaco the day after the Champions League final, Chelsea's owner already had all the information he needed.'

'I spent two days with him. He never once mentioned what he expected from me. Everyone in the club must feel we have a good relationship between us. If Mr Abramovich wants to be in on the training session that's fantastic. Or, if at the end of the match he wants to go to the dressing room, for me it's great. It's never a problem.'

Jose Mourinho? There was still so much to learn. And all sorts of astonishing and tricky games to play.

Chapter Nineteen
The Game

'Frank Lampard is the most improved English player of the last
two years and the prime is yet to come.'

JUNE 2004 POLL ON ENGLAND TEAM FOR THE 2006 WORLD CUP

Jose Mourinho gave no championship guarantees, but
he had made a good start, Chelsea 1 Manchester United 0.

Frank said that before the encounter the new manager
had told them: 'Let's have some fun.'

And they did. They certainly enjoyed themselves, despite
the absence of Arjen Robben and Damien Duff. Chelsea
scored an early goal through Eidur Gudjohnsen and then
kept the lid on United with the kind of display that so often
proved beyond Claudio Ranieri's Chelsea sides.

'Mentally we were a team,' said a delighted Mourinho
afterwards, but they were actually a good deal more than
that. They were determined, disciplined and defensively
strong, and what they lacked in invention they made up
for in intelligence.

Those in search of entertainment still found it, however.
The contest that developed between Mourinho and the

United fans provided anyone within earshot with an amusing alternative to the main event. Mourinho was surprised to discover opposing supporters in the seats immediately behind the dugouts at his new football home.

'In Portugal they are normally far away in a corner, behind a net,' said Mourinho. The proximity of rival fans allowed him to listen in on the 'inspired' invective which lurched between 'who the fuck are you?' to 'greasy foreigners'. Mourinho was cleverly polite: 'It was a beautiful song. Magnificent.'

And for him it probably was. Unfortunately, for his tormentors, their song debuted just as Gudjohnsen's fifteenth-minute goal arrived. What follows is an edited, 'pooled' report of the game:

'Chelsea caught Ferguson's men on the hop. What began with Quinton Fortune's failure to meet a clearance from William Gallas continued when the hapless Eric Djemba-Djemba left Didier Drogba free to direct Geremi's cross into the path of Gudjohnsen. Even then, though, it was still thanks to the hesitancy of Roy Keane, playing at centre-half, and Tim Howard that Gudjohnsen was first able to knock the ball over the advancing United goalkeeper before bundling it across the line.

'Djemba-Djemba deserved much of the criticism, however, and left Ferguson to reflect once again on the mistakes he has made in recent seasons. United's manager might have had a point when he reminded Mourinho that you need more than £89 million to win the title, but he forgot how costly it can prove when you spend your money unwisely.

'The nine players who were unavailable to Ferguson exposed the folly of some of his signings. Djemba-Djemba is no Eric Cantona, Fortune is poor, and in David Bellion and Diego Forlan he was hardly sending on the big guns as the search for an equaliser intensified. Mourinho said United's squad should be big enough to cope with so many injuries. It is because of some of the decisions Ferguson made twelve months ago that it is not.

'United enjoyed plenty of possession, but lacked any spark when they entered the final third, and for Alan Smith, in particular, that must have been frustrating. Ruud van Nistelrooy, Louis Saha and Cristiano Ronaldo cannot return soon enough.

'While Ferguson waits impatiently for his Olympians and injured players to come back, Mourinho can reflect proudly on a second win over United in less than six months.

'Ferguson accepted the invitation of a dodgy glass of wine off Mourinho – they sent through the cheap stuff – and perhaps he now realises that this precociously talented young pretender does possess something.

'Mourinho sent out a Chelsea side with four new faces and no wingers and they performed in a way that made them look anything but strangers. We will see more from Drogba, who possessed pace and power but not enough poise, and the two he left on the bench, Mateja Kezman and Ricardo Carvalho. Of that there is little doubt.

'The self-proclaimed "special coach" tried to appear charitable in victory before asking the assembled media if he could be excused to join his wife on her birthday. "We deserved a victory but they didn't deserve a defeat," he said. "I said as much to Ferguson." Ferguson no doubt appreciated his new rival's generosity.'

Yet, it is interesting to see the statistics of the game, especially recalling Mourinho's statements about possession.

These were the match facts:

CHELSEA		MANCHESTER UTD
41%	Possession	59%
3	Shots on target	1
4	Shots off target	9
3	Blocked shots	7
2	Corners	3
19	Fouls	9
4	Offsides	2
73%	Passing success	80%
49%	Tackle success	71%

The media frenzy followed the game. It was superb fun. For once they had Ferguson looking discomforted. And a young pretender to the Premiership throne. This was super stuff to report – and the newspapers took great advantage compiling reports like this on 16 August 2004: 'Jose Mourinho drew first blood against Sir Alex Ferguson in the Premiership title battle yesterday.'

Chelsea's Portuguese manager revealed that the 1–0 victory, secured by Eidur Gudjohnsen's goal, had been inspired by comments from Manchester United that a lack of team spirit at Stamford Bridge would cost them the title. On a day when champions Arsenal began with a comprehensive 4–1 win at Everton and were challenged by manager Arsène Wenger to go through the season unbeaten again, Mourinho took on United.

He said, 'Mikael Silvestre is a big player, but what he said about us having no time to create a team spirit was wrong. What we showed today was that we have a great spirit because this was a performance which proved it.

'I told my players that they have to be ready to fight for each other in every moment of a match because they will not ever dominate for ninety minutes and that is what we did today.'

Mourinho also pointed out that he has not had the luxury of years to prepare his players for the fight and could not resist reminding his rivals that he has done well so far even if he has spent almost £80 million on transfers.

'People always talk about the millions I have spent, but I would say look at Sir Alex Ferguson, who has been with his club for seventeen years, and Arsène Wenger, for seven years, and I have had seven weeks,' said Mourinho. 'If we can show the same qualities that we have against United after being together for three weeks then I think we have great hope for the season.'

Ferguson refused to be downbeat, despite the pain of losing to a manager with whom he has shared several verbal spats. He said, 'We were sloppy to concede the goal, but with the possession we had we might have done better. We had six chances and did not score, that was the difference.'

That summer Mourinho had been pursuing other sorts of chances. Chelsea had made seven high-profile signings in the summer transfer market. This was the line-up of those bought and the media judgements on them:

Ricardo Carvalho (£19.85m, Porto): His cool temperament and ability to second-guess the nippiest of forwards during Euro 2004 earned him the tag 'the new Beckenbauer' by a delighted Portuguese press. Should certainly be an improvement on the departed Marcel Desailly.

Paulo Ferreira (£13.2m, Porto): Another import from Mourinho's former club, another European Cup winner, but an unsteady showing at Euro 2004, particularly in the defeat by Greece in the opening game of the tournament, prompted a few questions about the size of his fee.

Mateja Kezman (£5m, PSV Eindhoven): Last season's influx of strikers failed to make any lasting impression at Stamford Bridge. Serbia and Montenegro striker Kezman could buck that trend, but his biggest battle at the start of the season will be to earn and keep a starting place in Mourinho's team.

Arjen Robben (£12m, PSV Eindhoven): Another player to put in mixed performances at Euro 2004, Holland's zippy winger was slowed somewhat in Portugal by a nagging hamstring injury. The fully fit version should make a bigger impression in the Premiership.

Tiago Mendes (£8m, Benfica): The third of the Portuguese imports, a midfielder with a big reputation back home, hence the £8 million fee. Like Kezman, will only really have the chance to shine if he gets a decent run in the starting line-up.

Petr Cech (£7m, Rennes): The Czech Republic's athletic goalkeeper will expect to oust Carlo Cudicini as Chelsea's No. 1. Whoever dons the gloves, though, Chelsea are guaranteed excellent cover from the bench, something they have lacked in previous years.

Didier Drogba (£24m, Marseilles): Had a superb season with Marseilles, but one season doesn't make a superstar. An undoubted talent, Drogba is an immensely strong forward and is powerful in the air, but the size of that price tag brings with it a weight of expectation that could be his toughest opponent this season. The Ivory Coast man won the Player of the Year award in France last season and scored five goals in the Champions League followed by four in the UEFA Cup as Marseilles reached the final. The most expensive striker in the Premiership has linked well with Eidur Gudjohnsen in Chelsea's pre-season matches. Now for the real thing.

Drogba and Petr Cech? Oh, what a power hindsight is. Frank Lampard had none of that when he talked about the summer of Mourinho's arrival, the summer of 2004 which Chelsea and he will always remember.

Frank recalls the meeting at the hotel in Manchester: 'Are you a winner?' But it was always as part of a team:

'The manager was clever because he didn't bring in superstars who had done it all and had nothing to prove.

'He brought in brilliant players, admittedly, very young and very hungry who want to work for the team. We haven't got a single individual who wants to be the main superstar. That's the club's strength.'

That and the lack of any fear whatsoever. Not many days after the defeat of Manchester United, Chelsea met Southampton at Stamford Bridge. They'd played four games and won four, the best start Chelsea had ever made to a season. The odds had dropped on the club bringing home the championship for the first time since Ted Drake's lads in 1955. For those inclined to gambling, hindsight is an even more terrible affliction.

Chelsea's next two matches were against Aston Villa away and Tottenham at home (both, as it turned out, goaless draws but, so importantly, not defeats) but Southampton were a hurdle.

Chelsea looked good as winners, being ahead of the game. There was much comment about how they would cope with being the underdog. They showed it against Southampton. James Beattie scored after just a dozen seconds, the fourth-fastest goal in Premiership history, but Chelsea's response was positive even after that slam-bang impact stunned the capacity crowd.

It was Joe Cole's misplaced pass that sold John Terry short, letting in Beattie, whose twenty-five-yarder carried over Petr Cech's head and under the crossbar. Going a goal down was a new experience, but Chelsea responded well, hitting back hard. Gudjohnsen might have equalised after four minutes, when he headed Frank's inviting left-wing cross wide from six yards, then Didier Drogba's left-footed shot was spilled by Antti Niemi, and Lampard, busily influential as ever, was unable to get a result from it.

When the roles were reversed, Frank fired over from twenty yards after Drogba's strong incisive run in the inside-left channel, then Frank was stopped by the first of two goal-line clearances by Anders Svensson. It was all Chelsea, and the inevitable equaliser, after thirty-four minutes came as no surprise, even if the scorer was. A corner from Frank, who had treatment to a cut around the eyebrow after fifteen minutes, was flicked on by Gudjohnsen, and Beattie turned the ball back past his own goalkeeper.

Chelsea's superiority was such that the only question was how many more they would score. Tiago would have doubled the margin with a header, but for Svensson's second intervention under his own crossbar, but the Saints' reprieve only lasted until forty-one minutes when Claus Lundekvam, challenging Drogba in the air, handled the ball.

Frank scored with the very legitimate penalty and was named Man of the Match. Everything, it seemed, was going according to plan. Everything, it appeared, was sweet.

The always enthusiastic Gary Lineker had his take on Frank and Chelsea's future with Jose Mourinho: 'I have been hugely impressed by the way Mourinho has quickly created a team spirit. It's noticeable how he speaks regularly of the British and Irish players in his side, which may be a clever diplomatic ploy on his part, but I prefer to think it's because they are so essential to the team's success. You could argue that Frank Lampard, John Terry and Damien Duff are their spine.'

Or you might say the men with lots of backbone.

Chapter Twenty

Trouble and Strife

'Lampard is making his fellow athletes
look like fair-weather joggers.'

CLIVE TYLDESLEY, DAILY TELEGRAPH, 18 SEPTEMBER 2004

The summer of 2004 brought new awakenings –
publicly at least – for Frank. Professionally, he was
seen as Chelsea and England's ace in the hole. His work
ethic had been superb.

'Someone at the Professional Footballers' Association
should have a word with Frank Lampard. If they can get
him to stand still long enough. While professional
footballers cramp and creak under the workload of too
many fixtures, Lampard is about to set a record for
consecutive appearances by an outfield player. He is
making his fellow athletes look like fair-weather joggers.'

That was Clive Tyldesley writing in the *Daily Telegraph* on
18 September 2004, who cleverly went on to point out,
'Three years ago he ran on at Stamford Bridge as a seventy-
third-minute substitute for Jimmy Floyd Hasselbaink against
Leicester. Like Forrest Gump, Frank just kept on running.

'Three weeks ago, Lampard had to leave the field against Southampton to have a head wound stitched. Global warming would not normally be enough to make Jose Mourinho lose his cool, but the Chelsea manager was snarling and glowering like Sir Alex at his angriest when Lampard's absence stretched to several minutes.

'His orchestra had suddenly gone flat without the conductor. The heart of his team were missing a beat while their pacemaker was in for repair. Lampard will be the first name on his teamsheet tomorrow. Even Claudio Ranieri knew not to tinker with Frank. The Chelsea squad rotate around their No. 8.

'Lampard's idea of a rest is playing for England at the European Championships. Since the start of last season [this is since 18 September 2004] he has clocked up seventy-nine games for club and country.

'Last December, he was actually substituted in a couple of Premiership games. That was his winter break. But here's the rub. The most prolific feature of the record run is the relentless improvement in Lampard's performance level.

'The more he plays the more he grows in stature and influence. He is making a myth of the hard labour of modern football. Lampard's record-breaking fun run is a reminder that football isn't necessarily bad for your health.'

But history can be. For someone's emotional wellbeing anyway. In the weeks before Tyldesley's glowing endorsement of his marathon-man dedication, details had surfaced of the Lampard family past.

TROUBLE AND STRIFE

It had been a difficult time for Frank and his family. And a quiet, private time. All involved are reluctant to discuss or go into pertinent details of the full background. There are indications that much of the story had been known in the East End for many years but, because of the admiration for Frank Senior, it was simply acknowledged rather than admitted. One family friend who approached Frank Senior about it found that what had been seen as a strong, loving relationship was, in reality, not quite the case.

On 4 July 2004 – American Independence Day – it was made public that Frank had a half-sister, Sophie, born a year after he was and a half-brother, John, born towards the end of his father's playing career. Sophie Butler, twenty-six in 2005, and John Butler, twenty-one in 2005, were born when Frank Lampard Senior was a West Ham star.

Their mother, Janet, was the other woman in his life for clearly some years. When he was approached about the situation in July 2004, by the *News of the World* who, astonishingly after all these years, had been informed by a family friend, he said, 'I accept what I did was wrong. This was an episode in my life that was some time ago and it is important that I draw a line under it now.'

The difficult revelations posed many questions. Did Harry Redknapp know about Janet Butler? Did Frank Senior's drinking mates at the Black Lion? 'In those days you kept some things under your hat. There was lots of stuff best left in the dressing room,' said Jeff Powell.

'Frank Senior would try it on with you. He was always

friendly to the girls,' said Patricia Brown, adding, 'But so were all the lads. Flirting was very much part of their game.'

But the report in the summer of 2004 made it clear that more than flirting had been involved. It was suggested to me that Pat Lampard knew about 'the other family', but that she lived with that knowledge in the interests of her own family's harmony. This was never confirmed or denied to me, despite many enquiries.

Most of all the answer was: it's the East End.

This *omertà* continued. What is known is that Sophie and John – Frank's half-siblings – live with their mother not that far away from their father's family home in Romford. Sophie, it was revealed, was conceived ten weeks after Frank Senior did his baby pictures with wife Pat and son Frank. John arrived nearly five years later. Frank Senior's name does not appear on either of his other children's birth certificates.

The *News of the World* quoted the family 'friend' as saying that Sophie and John had been 'hidden away'. It said that they lived in 'a modest terraced home' in Ilford in east London. It was also reported that Frank Senior did see Sophie (he appeared on her re-registered birth certificate in 1995) and John 'now and again'.

All of which makes us wonder how much subterfuge was going on within the family. Who knew what? As of March 2005, Frank had said nothing about his 'new' brother and sister. His father had said to the newspaper that reported the story, 'I made mistakes. I ask that I'm left alone with my family. I would like to thank the *News of the World* for dealing with this story so sensitively.'

TROUBLE AND STRIFE

The story of the Lampard 'secret family' had appeared at a complex time. The Frank Lampards, father and son, were appearing in television advertisements for Sainsbury's supermarkets with *Naked Chef* Jamie Oliver. Were they such a happy family unit?

Whatever family recriminations, it did not affect the professional Frank. He played as if his only concern in the world was scoring goals and winning.

And, despite the family turbulence, his life seemed to have settled. Gone were the gossip-column stories that he'd 'bagged' Liz McLarnon from Atomic Kitten or had been in this or that nightclub. He'd moved to a sumptuous apartment in Knightsbridge, close to Stamford Bridge, and he had found a meaningful girlfriend in Elen Rives. Of the Spanish girl he said, 'I'm happy and when you're happy in your life it makes everything easier. It's the first real relationship I've ever been in.

'Elen's a character. Good fun. She's got a fiery Spanish temperament, very fiery. She likes a sing-song, but she's a terrible singer. When we fell in love I'd never known anything like it before.'

Elen, who is close to Steven Gerrard's partner Alex Curran and John Terry's girlfriend Toni Poole, also became involved with one of Frank's important interests outside of football. He is a fervent supporter of the Teenage Cancer Trust and regularly visits their unit at the Middlesex Hospital. 'I just sit around and chat. The time passes very quickly. I'm not certain what I do – I hope I'm helping them along. But what I do doesn't seem very much.'

It is to the patients, many of them football fans, Frank

Lampard fans. The youngsters – like those in such serious hospital wards around the world – get pleasure from the interest taken in them, and the interest to these Middlesex Hospital children from someone like a world-renowned football star is immense.

What's telling is that he did not make one PR visit, but continues to do so and asks for contributions to be made in his name to the Teenage Cancer Trust (Teenage Cancer Trust, 38 Warren Street, London WIT 6AE) rather than accept most media fees. He has pledged himself as a lifelong supporter of the trust.

The ambition was to be an all-around winner.

Chapter Twenty-One

Odds-on

'Once Mourinho gets fully acclimatised, I think
there will be three of them knocking spots off each other:
Mourinho, Ferguson and Wenger. Jose is on the periphery at
the moment because he's been here for only five months.
But wait until he's won a trophy or two...'

SIR BOBBY ROBSON, 5 DECEMBER 2004

Events, as we know, control everything. But in early
2005 it looked as though Frank and Chelsea could
achieve a string of sporting miracles.

The day Frankie Dettori cost Britain's bookmakers £40
million, by winning every race at Ascot, began to haunt
them as Chelsea appeared as though they could possibly
remain unbeatable four times over.

If the 'unspeakable' had happened and Chelsea won the
quadruple, of the FA Cup, the Premiership, the Carling
Cup and the European Cup, the bookies faced a £20
million payout. When they were knocked out of the FA
Cup by Newcastle (1–0 and with Chelsea down to ten men
for much of the match and down to nine by the end) on
a bitterly cold, snow-swept day, 20 February 2004, the
bookies saved around £10 million. Bookmaking firms had
been slow to spot the Chelsea rollercoaster: Hills were

offering 400–1 on the Big Four at the beginning of the season. Ladbrokes offered 200–1.

There were no warning signals, because most of the bets being made were by small-time punters with a £5 or £10 long shot. But, once the totting-up started, the bookies realised they had a potential disaster looming.

By the middle of February 2005, they were quoting Chelsea as 9–2 favourites to win the European Cup, despite the fact that football die-hards expected Barcelona to trounce them over the two legs in the next round.

As bookies scrambled to lay off bets, the only person they could side with was Sir Alex Ferguson, that rather keen racing man in Manchester, who was hedging his bets in the hope that Chelsea might stumble in their particularly inclusive race.

International money men said that Chelsea will be one of the three richest clubs in Europe. The respected accountancy company Deloitte in their eighth Money League, published on 17 February 2005, said Chelsea, Manchester United and Arsenal would be the Big Three, overshadowing Real Madrid and Barcelona.

The Money League covered the 2003–04 season. Manchester United were Europe's wealthiest club with earnings of £171.5 million, slightly down on the year before. Chelsea, boosted by Abramovich's wealth, were fourth, behind Real Madrid and AC Milan. But they earned £143.7 million which made them, with Barcelona, the fastest growers in the financial race. Chelsea jumped six places in the wealth league, despite only having a 42,449-seat stadium and the report concluded, 'They will not think that future overall leadership is beyond them. With Chelsea's success and Arsenal's Emirates Stadium development, we can foresee a scenario where English clubs fill the top three places in the 2006–07 Money League.'

The report gave Britain's Top 10:

Revenue sources (in millions)

	Matchday	Broadcasting	Commercial	Average gate
Manchester Utd	61.2	62.5	47.8	67,500
Chelsea	53.6	56.4	33.7	39,700
Arsenal	33.8	59.8	21.4	36,600
Liverpool	26.4	33.5	32.4	41,800
Newcastle Utd	33.9	33.7	22.9	50,000
Celtic	34.7	16.1	18.2	56,000
Tottenham H	19.8	23.9	22.6	34,100
Manchester City	17.1	25.5	19.3	43,800
Rangers	24.2	7.5	25.4	47,200
Aston Villa	12.4	27.2	16.3	35,600

Europe's Top 20 Richest Clubs:
(Position for previous year in brackets)
Total revenues for 2003–04 in £ million

1. Manchester Utd (1)   171
2. Real Madrid (4)   156.3
3. AC Milan (3)   147.2
4. Chelsea (10)   143.7
5. Juventus (2)   142.4
6. Arsenal (7)   115

7. Barcelona (13)	112
8. Inter (6)	110.3
9. Bayern Munich (5)	110.1
10. Liverpool (8)	92.3
11. Newcastle Utd (9)	90.5
12. Roma (11)	72
13. Celtic (18)	69
14. Tottenham H (16)	66.3
15. Lazio (15)	65.8
16. Manchster City (–)	61.9
17. Schalke (14)	60.5
18. Marseilles (–)	58.3
19. Rangers (–)	57.1
20. Aston Villa (–)	55.9

Chelsea's first accounts under Ambramovich's ownership had shown just how costly it is to create and maintain an A-plus squad of players. The accounts showed that the Russian had invested £100 million of equity into the business and provided a further £115 million in the form of an interest-free loan with no specific repayment date. That is in addition to the original £59.3 million the club cost Abramovich.

In the year to June 2004, Chelsea made an operating loss of £13.1 million. The cash outflow for that period was £161.7 million – and not even Abramovich could sustain that consumption of cash forever.

Just over £175.1 million went in buying players from 2003 to 2004. Another £115.5 million was paid out in wages – Frank is one of the highest-paid players – bonuses and other remuneration. About thirty-five members of the Chelsea business earned £2 million – Chelsea is more generous than the world's biggest and most successful investment banks. But they will always need success on the pitch if Chelsea Football Club are to become a cash-generative, self-sustaining business.

And for all involved, players and fans, that is important, as unforeseen events and/or internal politics in Russia could possibly conspire to halt Abramovich's petrodollar flow. But that's supposing his $15 billion fortune is still behind the old Iron Curtain and not locked behind a string of numbers in a Zurich vault.

Chelsea is valued at £225.2 million, about a third of Manchester United, and will boost its finances through a 2005 sponsorship deal with adidas which is worth around £12 million over eight years. An equally lucrative shirt sponsorship arrangement was also concluded in the spring of 2005.

Chapter Twenty-Two
The Premiership Run

'You can't buy Frank Lampard handing the ball to
Kezman in those dying seconds...'

OLIVER HOLT, DAILY MIRROR, 6 DECEMBER 2004

For all the money involved, Frank's game was football.
He was exceedingly gracious, however. The Serbian
Mateja Kezman, bought by Chelsea from PSV Eindhoven
in the summer of 2004 for £5 million, had not been a
great performer. He'd scored just one goal – against West
Ham in the Carling Cup. Soon after he came on as a
substitute in the Chelsea v. Newcastle Premiership game
he hit the post. 'I almost cried when that didn't go in,'
recalled Chelsea's assistant manager Steve Clarke.

In the last moments of the game there was a penalty
awarded to Chelsea. Frank, the normal penalty taker,
handed the ball to Kezman, knowing what it would mean
to him to score his first Premiership goal in more than
marathon minutes of trying. Kezman delivered.

In that moment all the work that Mourinho had been
doing, the bonding, the 'Are you a winner' mantra came

good. 'When we were given the penalty I went to Frank and asked him,' remembered Kezman, adding, 'He gave me the ball because he knows how difficult it has been for me with no goals. Goals are my life. When you score twenty or thirty goals every year for the past seven or eight years and then just one in three months it's very hard.

'You could see our spirit after I scored. Every single player came to me. That was fantastic. That's our strength this season. That's how we can be champions. Frank Lampard did that for me...' And for the team which won 4–0 on the day.

Oliver Holt of the *Mirror* said in his match report, 'You can't buy Frank Lampard handing the ball to Kezman in those dying seconds. You can't buy the sight of every tired player in the Chelsea side engulfing Kezman in his happiness. You can't buy the gratitude he felt to his team-mates or the confidence such an audacious penalty will bring. Lampard's brilliance is becoming almost monotonous. He is producing match-winning performances week after week after week. He has become the complete player.'

But Frank had already been cast in that role in the run-up to the race for the Premiership. A glance back to Halloween in 2004, when Chelsea played West Bromwich Albion at the Hawthorns, shows that. It was all about character. They had suffered the 'nightclub' reporting of footballers' excesses (Adrian Mutu of Chelsea had been fired for taking cocaine and there had been lurid headlines about footballers' passion for casinos), but on the day won 4–1.

The game got this brief reaction: 'Chelsea put a bad news week behind them by drawing level with Arsenal at the top of the Premiership, scoring four goals for the second League game in succession.

'After all the spoiled-rich-boy stories about drug-taking and gambling excesses, the players got back to what they do best and ruthlessly exploited the shortcomings of opponents who are paying the inevitable price for fielding a First Division team in the Premier League.

'"We only win one–nil," chortled the blue-clad legions, ridiculing their team's early-season reputation as parsimonious scorers. Eidur Gudjohnsen, with a hat-trick, took the honours against Blackburn Rovers last week, but the goals were shared around this time, with one each from William Gallas, Gudjohnsen again, Damien Duff and Man of the Match Frank Lampard.

'Albion competed as best they could, but belong in a different league, which is where they are almost certain to be next season. They could not be faulted for effort under the caretaker managership of Frank Burrows, but are desperately short of Premiership quality, and Gary Megson's permanent replacement faces a task not so much uphill as vertical. The smart money is on Glenn Hoddle, but with no money to spend, he must be banking on reincarnation.

'"They are the best team we've played this season," Burrows said. "That man [Jose Mourinho] has done a very good job in a very short time. Nobody can give them a two-goal start, like we did. We got what we deserved."

'Mourinho was less impressed with his charges, and

deemed the first half the worst forty-five minutes of his tenure. The second half, he said, was a "completely different story" and Chelsea might have scored more. "We were dangerous every time we attacked," he said.

'Chelsea's three-man attack stretched West Brom early on, with Duff threatening on the left, but, as against Blackburn last week, it took them longer than they would have liked to translate possession into something worthwhile. It was in the forty-fifth minute that Lampard's corner from the right was met by John Terry, whose header from seven yards was turned over the line at negligible range by Gallas.

'Until that stage, Albion had acquitted themselves well. They produced the first attempt of the match, Nwankwu Kanu seeing his shot blocked by Terry, and their other striker, Wales's Robert Earnshaw, was not far away from twenty-five yards. Chelsea responded with a couple of characteristic salvoes from Lampard, but they rarely looked like making the breakthrough until Gallas scored.

'As against Blackburn, Arjen Robben, a half-time replacement for Joe Cole, was immediately in the thick of things. It was Claude Makelele, however, who threatened to double the margin before Gudjohnsen did so, after fifty-one minutes. Duff was the prime mover, delivering a cross that left the Iceland striker with a routine headed finish from six yards.

'Albion thought they had got themselves back in it within two minutes, when Petr Cech could only beat out a shot from Kanu and Zoltan Gera drove the ball straight back past the startled keeper. Chelsea, however, had other ideas, and restored their two-goal cushion almost immediately, courtesy of the latest example of Lampard's maturity into a midfielder of the highest class.

'The England man carried the ball some forty yards before picking out Duff with a peach of a pass. The Irishman made short work of the rest, cutting in and shooting confidently under Russell Hoult from twelve yards.

'At 3–1 it was game over. Albion continued to apply themselves, but theirs was now a forlorn task. Gera tested Cech with a decent shot from twenty yards, but Robben produced a similar attempt at the other end, then set up Chelsea's fourth, after eighty-one minutes. The Dutch winger squared the ball to Lampard who, from twenty yards, thumped it past Hoult's right hand. The scorer was promptly substituted, his job well done again.

'The blue legions broke off from choruses of "Super Frankie Lampard" to tell their hosts: "You're going down." It was hard to argue on either count.'

Chapter Twenty-Three
Frankly Speaking

'Frank's the winner.'
JOSE MOURINHO, FEBRUARY 2005

Frank Lampard was acknowledged as one of England and Chelsea's greatest players in 2005. You can't, of course, put it all down to hard work, to that extra training, the parental encouragement and work ethic. There's the 'it' factor, the talent, the magic, that has to be there. As Claudio Ranieri said, 'If the marble is good I can improve the player.'

In Frank's case it seemed more solid gold than marble considering his incredible improvement and rise to distinction in international football. A year earlier he was no more than a cameo player for Sven-Goran Eriksson, now he was one of the star turns. And even more so for Jose Mourinho.

With their new leader, Frank believed there were few limits for both his and his team's future. As we know, the manager spells out almost everything for his players except how to breathe. Frank pointed out, 'In training, everything is now done with a ball. Before, a lot of it was physical stuff with the fitness coach. Under Mourinho, virtually everything we do is intended to replicate a match situation. That has helped the players technically and made us more tactically aware.

'The work we do with a ball, day in day out, is the foundation of the team's strength. We look strong and solid because we hammer away at getting it right every day in training. The organisation is becoming ingrained.

'It's not that we've just got the one way of playing, but if we do change we really do know what we're doing because it has been mapped out beforehand. In the build-up to the game the manager will have prepared us for every possibility. He'll say, "If this happens, we might change to this."

'It's never off-the-cuff, as it was under Ranieri, it's always something that has been pre-planned. The manager knows how productive free-kicks and corners can be. If you get it right, the delivery, the routine and the movement, you'll score goals.

'In my case, I'm taking free-kicks and corners which I was never entrusted with before. He has given me that responsibility, it's something I've added to my game and it has made me believe in myself even more. He is bringing out the best in me. What I haven't got is as many goals and that's something that bothers me, because I think like a striker – if I haven't scored I'm not happy no matter how well I've played. I do need to be among the goals.

'We spend more time on that than we did under

Claudio Ranieri, not just on the training pitch but in team meetings, after watching the opposition.

'There is a rule book. But because I came back late after the Euros I didn't get my copy until two weeks later. The papers made a lot about its contents – more than is actually in there. There are guidelines, governing punctuality and the like, but they are not as strictly applied as people have made them out to be.

'There is one main rule, which is that you behave like a professional at all times. Otherwise, if you are late for training or whatever, he will always listen to your reason. He doesn't crack down with an iron fist straight away.

'As regards socialising, it's not as the press reported it, that we must be in by midnight on such and such a day or 1am on another. What he is saying is: "As long as you're sensible, and go out at the right times, that's fine by me, but if you go out drinking the day before a match, or the night before training, you're not going to be able to train or play as I want you to."

'He's very approachable. I was comfortable with him right from the start, and I think all of us felt that way. He gave me confidence. We've gone from 4–4–2 to 4–3–3 and we keep the ball a lot more. There are times when we want to take the sting out of games, and now we can really do that.'

Mourinho had a clear idea from the start how he wanted Frank to fit into his Chelsea team, 'He can remain the same individually, but I want to change him in relation to the team, like we did with Deco at Porto. It all depends on what the team needs from him. If one day I tell Frank I don't want him to be a box-to-box player, but to hold back, he has to adapt to our needs.

'We put a stamp on a player and say "he's this type", but sometimes that player has to be different. He was used to playing side by side with Makelele, but I've got him playing a different line to Makelele.'

Frank says his boss is happy winning, even 1–0. 'We all are. The manager does like to play good football, he's not one of those who wants to defend, content to play unattractive football and nick a result. He'd be happier, obviously, winning 3–0, but 1–0 will do as well.

'I've got the licence to get forward whenever I want to, as long as I can get back when needed as well. It's nice to have the insurance of "Maka" [Makelele] behind me. Because he's always there, I can push on.

'For our first two games we played with a midfield diamond but, since then, we've been 4–3–3. People said Joe Cole was playing in the hole, but he wasn't. He was pushed up on the left, but could drift inside when he wanted to. Joe's not naturally left-sided, so he tended to come in a lot, as does Eidur [Gudjohnsen] on the right.

'I think we're better balanced when Damien Duff plays. He gives us more width because going wide is his natural instinct. Once you have that width, there's the threat to the opposition that you can spread it wide, they have to guard against that, and space opens up for me to run into.'

He has the stature of an England player now and wears it well. 'Before the Euros, I'd played twenty times, but often as a substitute and you don't feel comfortable until you're starting games. It's only after you've had a run in the side that you start to feel that you belong.

'That feeling flowed through me in Portugal and now I view the England situation entirely differently. I'm part of the team and expect to be starting.'

And that has been the dream since his father first threw a ball at his feet.

Chapter Twenty-Four

Frank Talk

'Mourinho's a breath of fresh air. Some people say
he's a flash bastard, but you can only get away with
that if you're really good.'

GEORGE BEST, 13 FEBRUARY 2005

Chelsea still had a chance at four trophies when
George Best focused on their hopes. One thing he was
certain about was that his beloved Manchester United
would not win the Premiership. 'Never mind the maths.
When you've got to rely on others losing, you might as
well turn it in. You can't go on hoping Chelsea might drop
a point here or there. It doesn't work that way. Chelsea are
running away with it. Rightly so, the way they play.

'And Jose Mourinho's a breath of fresh air. Some people
say he's a flash bastard, but you can only get away with
that if you're really good. Sure he's spent a lot, but a lot of
managers spend big money. It's what you get with it that
counts. Me, I love him. You see, he does the little things
well. He gets his players to throw their shirts to the crowd.
Or Scunthorpe turn up for a cup game and he makes them
feel welcome. He puts on a show for them.

'Some of the great ones did that. Sir Matt [Busby], Shankly, Nicholson, Stein, Clough. They all tried to do the little things well. It's important. And he's got an awesome side. I mean, even when they're poor, the worst they get is a point. That's the way you win the title.'

The furore over the so-called approach by Chelsea to Arsenal's Ashley Cole brought merriment from Best. 'They say they're tapping people, is that right? Nothing new there. They tapped me once. It wasn't what you'd call subtle. They just told the press they'd like me in their team. No big deal. They weren't the only ones. I had both the Milan clubs, Real Madrid, one or two others. But they were all wasting their time. We were winning things, weren't we? I mean, we won the big one, the European Cup. You couldn't leave a team like that.

'Still, it was interesting the way they went about it. You'd see them in the players' lounge and they'd give you a card and say, "If you're ever in Madrid or Milan, perhaps we could have lunch?" Tricky people these foreigners. Chelsea were different. They just came right out with it.'

Best, like many others, admires Mourinho's man-management. Gordon Strachan, who as player-coach with Coventry famously and sympathetically put a comforting arm around Frank when the West Ham crowd welcomed him with that spiteful loud booing, said, 'You might not see managers as agony aunts but, oh dear, some of the things we've heard. Some of the kids come from tough homes. They have lots of problems.

'Footballers get the blame for yobbish behaviour but, if you think about it, they're yobs before they get here. If you've got a yob and he meets money, it's a hell of an explosive combination. To be a good coach, like Mourinho, is like being a good doctor. You take an oath to make people better. It's the manager's responsibility to teach young players respect because, if he could do that to me, he could do it to coaches, team-mates, the opposition. I always told every player of mine to come to me if they had a problem.'

One of his youth players once nutmegged him in a training match and mouthed 'Nuts' at him. Strachan admits he went ballistic and gave the player some of Sir Alex Ferguson's infamous 'hairdryer' treatment. 'If some of these kids don't respect their mum and dad, managers, authority of any kind, then we get blamed for not disciplining them. It's difficult, but it's part of a manager's job.'

Maybe he still had the festive spirit, but it was in early January 2005 that Mourinho played happy host to Scunthorpe (League Two) in the incident George Best recalled. Chelsea did the job on the field (they won 3–1), but the manager won the good-grace stakes. The man who created a career out of influencing people was now winning friends, too. He gave the freedom of Stamford Bridge to opponents almost seventy places beneath him in the football pecking order.

When Scunthorpe arrived on Saturday morning to familiarise themselves with the stadium, Mourinho acted as their tour guide. Before they left, he presented them with his scouting report that had contributed to their downfall. Scunthorpe manager Brian Laws said, 'Mourinho treated us like kings and we nearly took a ransom. When we shook hands at the end he said, "With that luck we will win the championship."

'Maybe he can be a bit arrogant and bigheaded, but he has a personality like Brian Clough and I say that by way of a huge compliment because Brian was a legend. Jose made my players feel very special. People call him ruthless and rude, but that isn't the Jose Mourinho I met. He took us into their dressing room and told us to talk with everyone, get shirts and autographs. He made it one of the great days for all of us.'

There has been much debate about what's been going on in Frank's world at Chelsea, all in a very short time compared to the long history of the club. Many have their view. John Hollins has a unique one. He's been a player, coach and manager at Chelsea in very different days to the ones he has witnessed in 2004 and 2005.

He was in charge of Chelsea in the debt-ridden old days and once had to spend £50 of his own money to get the Stamford Bridge grass cut. Jose Mourinho can afford five times as much on a bottle of red wine to share with Sir Alex Ferguson, but Hollins, who also had to sell five talented youngsters for a total of £250,000 to help keep the club afloat, has no hard feelings.

He talked before Chelsea's FA Cup mishap at Newcastle, but his thinking was, and is, extremely valid. 'Winning all four trophies is on, of course it is. It requires consistency and Chelsea have proved they have that. The attitude must be right and they have that, too. It requires a marvellous team spirit and it's obvious in the way they play that they have that.

'You need class players and Chelsea have them in abundance. And, perhaps most importantly, it is essential that the team is run by a manager the players respect and who respects the players. Well, in Jose Mourinho, they certainly have such a man. And, if they survive Barcelona, everything is possible.'

Hollins led Chelsea into more battles than any player in the club's history during the sixties and seventies. But while they excelled in the cups – Hollins played in the famous FA Cup final replay victory over Leeds United in 1970 – a lack of consistency was their downfall.

While the contrast between the resources available to the two men as managers is astonishing, Hollins can see similarities between the Mourinho era and his own playing days. 'We were a team in the real sense. We had the right attitude and so do Mourinho's team. The first Chelsea team I played in as a seventeen-year-old, the 1964 side, had Terry Venables, Eddie McCreadie, Barry Bridges and George Graham. We were young and confident and could outrun anyone else in the First Division.

'Isn't that an outstanding quality of the present team, too, to run and work for each other, to want to play, no, to *desire* to play for Chelsea?

'Yes, he has the money he needs to buy the very best. I remember how difficult things were when I was manager. Once I couldn't believe how long the grass was getting. I asked why it hadn't been cut and was told they owed money on the mower and weren't allowed to use it. I gave the groundsman £50 of my own money and told him to go out and buy anything that would solve the problem.

'But it's not only the money. Mourinho also has scientific knowledge that was not available to us. For example, as players we used to have a big steak and rice pudding before every match. We now know it takes five hours to digest that sort of meal, but we weren't aware of that then, yet in a couple of hours we'd be out there running like hares.

'It helps when you know. Jean Tigana, for example, when he was coach at Fulham, used to insist on regular hands, feet and teeth examinations. You can discover a lot from the condition of teeth. If we had a toothache we'd just ask for a tot of whisky, but it wouldn't stop us playing.

'Now if you have so much as a sniffle you are left out – although I noticed John Terry, who has been outstanding, coughing hard in the warm-up before the Middlesbrough game. I thought then that he was taking a big chance if he had failed to tell them he wasn't 100 per cent.'

With the run-up to the Premiership, the debate went on and on about Chelsea, the world's most talked-about team. The ongoing question – could money buy success? There were comments from specialists to fans, even non-Chelsea fans like Edie May-Bedell in Leeds. 'I support Leeds, so know the trauma of what can happen when a team tries to buy its way to the top. However, I am fed up of the anti-Chelsea bias in the media.

'So, they have lots of money. What do you think Manchester United and Arsenal have spent – a shiny sixpence and half a crown? It seems ludicrous to set a limit on what is an acceptable amount of obscene wealth. Are millions good and super-millions bad?

'We should welcome a team that can at last break the dominance of United and Arsenal. The implied criticism that Chelsea are only top because of Roman Abramovich's millions is both wrong and insulting to the hard work done by Jose Mourinho and his team. Do they have too much money? Yes, but so do all top teams.'

Chelsea member Matthew White added, 'For years we have been disliked (hated would be so over dramatic) for the sole reason of a thorough disliking for Ken Bates. To an extent I can understand this. None of this really mattered because for twenty-six years Chelsea never won anything and never seriously challenged for the League title.

'Now things have changed and suddenly we are becoming everybody's punch bag. Yes, we have spent money, but so have Man Utd and others for years. I don't remember cries of Liverpool being bad for the game when, already the No. 1 side in the country in the 1980s, they went out and bought John Barnes and Peter Beardsley, two of the most sought-after properties of the time.

'Is the introduction of Robben, Cech, Makelele and Drogba bad for the game? Above all, is Mourinho bad for the game? Surely he is the best thing that has happened to the Premiership this season. Forget about Fergie and Wenger's handbags – Mourinho is the man and blue is the colour.'

Sol Campbell of Arsenal was, understandably, not of the same view. 'In my time at Arsenal I've noticed anyway that we don't really kick on until the last ten or fifteen games. Some players, some teams, run out of steam.

'You've got someone (Roman Abramovich) who doesn't care about money, so of course you can get players from all over the world. Then you've got a new manager coming in. Everyone wants to work hard. It's normal. But no one can keep up that kind of tempo all season. It's impossible.'

Not so partisan was David Platt, who won the UEFA Cup with Juventus, and believed England's best chance of winning the Champions League in 2005 was with Chelsea. 'Mourinho has proved he knows what it takes. The most attacking teams generally find it hard to win the Champions League. If it means playing a bit more negatively, Mourinho will say fine. He will do anything, change anything, to win.'

After Chelsea beat Newcastle 4–0 in December 2004, Newcastle manager Graeme Souness said, 'They are a team filled with top players and they are the team to catch now. But you'd be a fool to say nobody can catch them. I don't think people in Manchester or north London think the game is up yet. But I'm still a bit shell-shocked because 4–0 was harsh.'

And in the same month, Alex Ferguson was calling Frank's constant performances 'freakish' and clearly regarded Chelsea as the biggest threat to his team. After using his mind games to undermine Arsenal in previous weeks, the United boss turned his attentions to Mourinho's Premiership leaders by questioning whether the Londoners had the stamina to stay the course as they looked to become champions for the first time in half a century.

Ferguson said, 'Chelsea will go close in both the

Premiership and the Champions League, but the thing is that so far the only thing they have done is go close in things. Jose Mourinho has done well so far. He has got Chelsea in a position where everybody is now wondering how they are going to be caught.

'It will be a hard task to catch them, but the key thing is that as a team they have no experience of winning the games that really, really matter like we have and like Arsenal have. Chelsea will get a blip – I have no doubt that they will lose a game or two.

'And there have been a lot of clubs before Chelsea who have looked in control all season only to see the title fly out of the window in March. Both ourselves and Arsenal have been through the mill for a number of years now and that's the advantage we have over Chelsea.

'Mourinho has surprised me by picking strong teams for the League Cup. Maybe it was to be expected in the quarter-final because it was a local derby against Fulham, but I have heard that they are now talking about winning all four competitions. I don't know about that. My maxim is that it is a good achievement to win one trophy every year and anything else is a bit greedy.'

Chelsea were definitely that as both the weeks and games ticked on...

Chapter Twenty-Five
The Six-day War

'Chelsea could go out and buy all the superstars in the
world, players who have been there and done it. But maybe
Jose prefers younger players, with hunger and fire in
their belly. We are ready to start winning now...'

JOE COLE ON 26 FEBRUARY 2005, THE EVE OF THE CARLING CUP FINAL

Frank Lampard had plenty of fire in his belly. And a
great incentive to win honours with Chelsea.

He had only a 2002 FA Cup loser's medal (Arsenal won
the day 2–0 on 5 May 2002) and an acknowledgement for
winning the InterToto Cup as 'medals' for his senior career.

For that other Upton Park graduate Joe Cole, the only
trophy proof of his remarkable skill was the FA Youth Cup
he won with West Ham.

But they and their team-mates were producing
breathtaking football, to a backdrop of a settled shape and
a strong defence, choreographed by Jose Mourinho;
Chelsea's spirit was outstanding and Frank and John Terry
were named daily in the newspapers as contenders for
Footballer of the Year.

The oddball was the manager. Jose Mourinho was in
charge of arguably the biggest and strongest football club

in the world and, at times, one wondered if he believed that his personality should match that.

Only the gloom-merchants were dismayed by Mourinho's swagger – wasn't it about time a new force unsettled the dominance of Arsenal and Manchester United? He was the new, bright spark in the game. And his electricity was everywhere. But in the key, last week of February 2005, he seemed overcharged.

At times it was embarrassing. The manager who had ridden into town like Clint Eastwood, with the stubble if not the cheroot, to take over the town suddenly found himself looking lost. And losing crucial football games.

Sir Alex Ferguson has not been in the game and winning for so long not to have a crystal ball; his predicted 'blip' for Chelsea did happen.

Against Newcastle United in the FA Cup he made a dramatic triple substitution at half-time. He lost Wayne Bridge to a foot injury. His ten remaining men lost the match.

Blip.

From the cold and despondency of Newcastle, Frank and the others flew off to Spain for their confrontation with that nation's great team, Barcelona. Chelsea, Mourinho and the team had taken much stick after the defeat at Newcastle. The way the coverage went it seemed as though they had lost their lives and not just a football game. Frank said, 'Everyone's been waiting for it to happen, to make a big deal out of it. It comes with the territory of being a team who win a lot. I think Arsenal probably got it when they finally lost a game.'

Yet there were more problems in Barcelona. The sending-off of Didier Drogba at the Nou Camp was a controversial moment which changed the face of a game that Chelsea had got back into but had lost, 2–1. For all the commentators, of course, it was blip number two.

Chelsea were sitting on top of a well-financed pedestal. According to some reports, the Chelsea squad and their leader were cracking up.

But then the focus shifted to the manager again. Mourinho, dragging the play away from his team's performances, put himself into the spotlight: one that has rarely captured his bad side. He complained that Frank Rijkaard, the much-liked and respected Barcelona coach, had talked with the referee at half-time (and this is something of a Mourinho obsession) and also that he'd been kicked in the backside (later denied) by one of Rijkaard's assistants in a tunnel incident. He then refused to attend the post-match press conference.

It was like his run-in with Sir Alex Ferguson in January 2005, whom he accused of influencing the match referee at half-time in the Carling Cup semi-final. 'I believe he was just playing games,' said BBC pundit Gary Lineker adding, 'I am fairly sure he was just trying to sneak what tiny advantage could.'

Maybe it *was* tactics, diverting attention from the scoreline, from his lads. Yet, he had made a series of mistakes. The three-man substitution against Newcastle was fatal – Chelsea were out of the FA Cup.

And the 'special one' had failed to deliver against Barcelona, although, as he was quick to point out, it was only leg one. 'We are not a club with a culture of winning like Manchester United, Juventus, Milan and Real Madrid, clubs who have had years to construct a team.

'If you want to have a short memory or put pressure on Chelsea, just mention the amount of money spent over the last two years and demand more victories. But there is no reason to be unhappy. They can't talk about blips.'

For Frank it was an unsettling week, but one which he had mentally prepared for. He is so steeped in football and in the history of the game that he knows it's not just a beautiful one but also a cruel one.

The Newcastle defeat was a shock, Barcelona a hurdle. Bobby Robson famously said of the Spanish city which competes with Madrid for attention, 'Barcelona is a nation without a country and Barca is its army.'

Frank's girlfriend Elen Rives, a Catalan, is fiercely proud of her area's football club and a supporters of the *azul granas*, the scarlet and blues; diplomatically, the woman in the life of Chelsea's vice-captain never revealed which team she was cheering for.

More importantly for Frank and Chelsea was whether they, as a side, used to the constant knockabout of Premiership football, could deal with future European pressure where wins develop more often through science than chance, where possession of the ball is a way of life, not a momentary thing.

For after Newcastle and Barcelona their war games continued against Liverpool in a head-on, one-off clash for the Carling Cup. It was Frank's big chance for a solid silver trophy.

Chapter Twenty-Six
The Race for Glory

'Frank Lampard is a fine player. He's very creative, he changes directions and he's cute. His goals are a big bonus. The Chelsea players are confident right now. They enjoy playing and doing all the positive things.'

SIR BOBBY CHARLTON, 26 MARCH 2005

The blue corner of the Millennium Stadium was packed with excitement and celebration as Chelsea's captain John Terry and his number two Frank Lampard led their squad in a cavalcade of self-acclaim. Up in the stands there was a banner shouting: 'Mourinho for Prime Minister.'

After winning the Carling Cup, the Chelsea manager had greater plans than that. It's like the old story about Bill Shankly when he was manager of Liverpool. He was asked whether football was life or death to him and he replied, 'No, it's much more important than that.'

Roman Abramovich nervously watched his players take on a determined Liverpool after their shaky week in Newcastle and Barcelona.

And it was a nail-biting beginning for Chelsea fans. After only forty-five seconds Fernando Morientes skilfully moved the ball to the far post and John Arne Riise put a powerful volley into the favourites' net. And for nearly eighty minutes, what looked like an eternity for Abramovich in the stand and Mourinho on the line, Liverpool remained one goal up in the Cup final.

It was dramatic movement throughout. Chelsea held possession of the ball, but kept being blocked by Liverpool's defence. They had the ball, but Liverpool had the goal.

Frank got the better of Steven Gerrard as John Terry acted as commander-in-chief on the field. But no result.

The frustrated Mourinho kept shouting at his squad, 'Come on. Come on!'

Mourinho took off Gallas and substituted Kezman, the score-starved import Frank had helped get his first Premiership goal, and the game changed. Suddenly.

Frank swooped through the middle of the field and over the halfway line when he was brought down. Paulo Ferreira belted in the free-kick which Liverpool's captain Gerrard helped into the net with an own goal. It brought an obvious response following all the transfer talk.

Was this Gerrard's first goal for Chelsea? It was an important one.

The equaliser set off a Chelsea clamour, but Mourinho turned to the crowd and put his finger to his lips signalling 'Hush'. Later, he said it was to silence the British press, but the crowd safety officer decided the Chelsea manager had to go – banished to the television company's control room. That's where he watched the rest of the game. The only commentary was him shouting at the television set.

Extra time brought out the best in Chelsea and tiredness in Liverpool. Even Liverpool's anthem 'You'll Never Walk Alone' couldn't get the Kop squad's legs working full-time. You could see them slowing down.

Frank clapped his hands time and time again, cheering on his team-mates. Up in the stands Abramovich had his head in his hands at times. Mourinho? Presumably he was still shouting at the silent television.

In what seemed like a moment, we were in the second half of extra-time. Glen Johnson, that other Upton Park graduate, had come on for Joe Cole, and it was his throw-in which allowed value-for-money Drogba the chance to score from close range in the 107th minute. Five minutes later and Frank was in the thick of the action.

His free-kick was hammered against Dudek by Gudjohnsen and, in the moments of muddle, the fresh-legged Kezman was there to poach, to sneak Chelsea's third goal over the line. A minute later Antonio Nunez headed in Gerrard's free-kick, but it didn't matter any more for Liverpool.

Chelsea had won the Carling Cup.

In a pantomime sequence, Mourinho was escorted by a Football League lawyer from his banishment and wandered around the pitch congratulating and hugging his players. He shook hands with everyone – including Steven Gerrard.

There was talk of fines and investigations, but for most people in Cardiff all that had mattered was the result. 'You cannot underestimate how important winning the Carling Cup was to Chelsea. If there was ever the case of the performance not mattering, this was it,' said commentator Alan Hansen after the game, adding, 'It was massive for Chelsea. They have come off the back of two defeats, they have lost a goal in the first minute of a Cup final and the manager goes on a walkabout among Liverpool supporters. If they had been beaten by Liverpool, even on penalties, it would have been catastrophic.

'If they had lost for the third time in a week it's conceivable they would have ended up with nothing. It's a funny thing pressure. It was starting to build up on Chelsea, but the result in Cardiff has washed away much of it. It makes a massive difference to them mentally.'

Mourinho had been shuffled off stage at the Millennium Stadium and Frank and John Terry, the English yeomanry with Joe Cole among the imported goal-seekers, had headed the cast, put on the show with the rest of the team.

And, as they touched, kissed and held up the Cup, soaked in sweat and champagne spray, the second leg with Barcelona was only days away. As was what Alex Ferguson's calls 'the squeaky bum' period as the Premiership raced to a conclusion.

Frank Lampard knows rather too well the often cruel world of football. For now he could enjoy the glory. He's learned it's best to do that when you can. And for Chelsea, in its celebration centenary year, it was a golden time of jubilation. Especially with their superb battle against Barcelona which, against the odds given by the doomwatchers, was a legendary night for Frank and for

Chelsea. And also for Jose Mourinho, who had been dubbed 'the gobby Potugeezer' and 'the little dictator of Stamford Bridge' by Chelsea's rivals.

Frank's mentor had become a public favourite. The England manager's great supporter David Davies looks set to depart the Football Association in 2006, and Sven Goran-Eriksson could possibly be going with him. Sven may even go before, depending, of course, on 'events'. What would the popular vote be on Jose taking over the England squad? It's a watch-this-space debate.

This echoes what Jose Mourinho said after his team's 2–1defeat by Barcelona in their first encounter of the Champions League. You could not ask for much more excitement from the second half of a very potent encore.

The evening of 8 March 2005 was a momentous one at Stamford Bridge. Frank and the lads had gone in handicapped by the away-goal rule. That hurdle started to diminish just seven minutes after kick-off when Eidur Gudjohnsen scored Chelsea's first goal (1–0, Agg 2–2). Nine minutes later Frank, on a brilliant evening for him, added a second from close range following up Joe Cole's cross (2–0, Agg 3–2).

Two minutes on, it was the softly spoken, amiably shy Damien Duff's turn, with Joe Cole's help, sweeping the ball through the legs of the advancing Barcelona keeper Victor Valdes (3–0, Agg 4–2). All looked good and then suddenly it was a hands-over-the-eyes moments for the Chelsea fans as well as for Roman Abramovich.

The Spanish side retaliated with a penalty from

Ronaldinho (3–1, Agg 4–3) which the Brazilian star followed eleven minutes later with a clever 20-yard delivery which put Barcelona ahead on away goals at half time (3–2, Agg 4–4).

It was heart-stopping. On the terraces, the crowd were looking away as the drama became more intense. Frank, who is always outstanding and sets the ongoing examples of tackling back and the teamwork ethic, had said after the so-called 'blips' that they had just been unlucky and added, 'We'll bounce back.'

This evening they did just that with Frank's friend John Terry providing the 'boy's own' moment. Terry headed a precious winner from a corner fourteen minutes from time to make it (4–2, Agg 5–4). Terry had run in to meet Damien Duff's out-swinging corner with an inspirational flip of his neck to put the header directly from his pale receding forehead past Victor Valdes. As the Stamford Bridge home brigade cheered the world, rival fans shouted that Ricardo Carvalho had hampered Valdes, and the atmosphere was ecstatic, exciting and worrying all at once.

The final whistle from referee Pierluigi Collina saw the start of chaotic scenes. Barcelona manager Frank Rijkaard and his players took exception to a crowing response to victory by Jose Mourinho's scout, Andre Villas. Rijkaard was angry with Villas; Samuel Eto'o and Ronaldinho did the macho thing and also remonstrated causing stewards to intervene. Eto'o, who claimed he was called a monkey, allegedly spat at a steward. The row spilled over into the tunnel.

Barcelona fans then became involved, pelting Mourinho

with plastic bottles for blowing kisses at them and launching missiles at Roman Abramovich. The Chelsea owner ignored them – he was intent on reaching the home dressing room.

Rijkaard tried to play down the tunnel incident and said, 'It was not a big deal. You know what it's like when emotions run high. Some guy, I have no idea who he was, came over at the final whistle and said something. He insulted our bench. People show their emotions sometimes.'

Mourinho, who had all but danced across the pitch after what was a great evening and victory, said after he hugged Frank and the team, 'We are in the quarter-finals and we have beaten the team who are – according to the press – the best in the world.

'Any result that put us through would have been fantastic. We faced a very good team, we were losing 2–1 before the start and we were without some of our best attacking players [the injured Arjen Robben and suspended Didier Drogba]. The way the players did it in the second half was fantastic.

'We scored four and should have scored six or seven. Barca could have had three, four or five.

'The football was magnificent. But over the 180 minutes I think the best team go through. Until the last second, if they score we go out. It was a game full of emotion.'

Chapter Twenty-Seven

Gladiator

'Lampard is one of the big, big midfielders in the world. He could play in any team.'

SVEN-GORAN ERIKSSON, 25 MARCH 2005

As World Cup 2006 hotted up, Frank had played in more senior football games than anyone in the Premiership. He had missed only two games for Chelsea in two seasons. They were in an FA Cup tie at home to Scunthorpe and a League Cup fixture with Notts County. He had been suspended for the Scunthorpe game.

That West Ham work-ethic upbringing was evident on 26 March 2005, when he appeared for England against Northern Ireland. His Chelsea colleague Joe Cole got the headlines but Frank helped him make them with a top rating as a performer on the day. He was dominant throughout the match, set up Michael Owen's goal and got his reward with a goal from his deflected shot in the 62nd minute. He believed there could have been more that day. 'My main aim is to keep shooting, because if you don't shoot you won't get that stroke of luck.

'I'm very pleased with my goals for England. I just keep trying to get into positions and keep shooting. Against Northern Ireland I had a bit of luck with a deflection but if you don't shoot, you don't score. You have to keep plugging away, looking for the openings.

'Scoring goals is a big part of my game. I get tired at times in games but if you are an experienced player you can save your legs a bit for a period and then come back strong again. I used to bomb forward all the time at West Ham and get in the box all the time, but I've matured and I've learned the right time.

'I've learned. All good teams have the ruthless streak. We play at Chelsea week in and week out and we don't panic if we don't score in the first half. Facing defensive teams is not easy and you might dominate games but not necessarily score six in the first half.'

His goal against Northern Ireland – his eighth for England in thirty-one games – put him alongside World Cup winner Alan Ball who won seventy-two caps and Glen Hoddle who was awarded 53. He still has to get a few more in the net to get close to Sir Bobby Charlton's England record of 49 goals in 106 appearances.

But he's getting there. His performances for England in March 2005 won him plaudits from his sport's most influential figures and headlines like LAMPARD JOINS THE ELITE and WINNING ETHOS DRIVES ON TIRELESS LAMPARD.

The 4–0 victory at Old Trafford had followed a day's shopping in Manchester for Frank and his team-mates. Given the afternoon off by Sven-Goran Eriksson Frank, John Terry and David Beckham took their gold and black heavyweight credit cards to the High Street in Manchester with Frank spending up at Flannels. They have the money. The next day the *Sunday Times* in London published a Young List of the richest footballers in England, aged under thirty. Frank Lampard and John Terry were positioned at joint number nine, each with a fortune of £8 million. So why shouldn't they be smiling?

They were easily spotted in their England 'sweats' but Frank handled the attention and the photographers with aplomb. It appears he will never suffer or attract the madness of the attention his England captain David Beckham gets. Maybe it's simply an attitude he has: there's access and then a clear STOP sign. It can only go so far.

While Frank and John Terry enjoyed the crowds, David Beckham had arranged for the adidas (the brand he endorses for £3 million a year) store in Manchester to close to the public for three-quarters of an hour so he could browse in privacy. He'd arrived in his Hummer H-2 all-terrain vehicle with VII, his trademark number seven, on the wheels. Moth to a flame, anyone? The crowds were soon massing around the store in the city's Triangle Centre. A camera was pointed at Beckhamn and he yelled, 'Don't take pictures of me!' He ran out of a back exit.

Meanwhile, Frank and John Terry and their shopping packages were winging their way through the Saturday afternoon shoppers.

And why not?

Frank Lampard thrives on the challenge. And he is confronting many of them with Chelsea and also with his national side as they approach the 2006 World Cup, the fortieth anniversary of when England last won that competition.

There are many Lampard family recollections – and lessons – down that particular memory lane, not least the ghosts of Bobby Moore and co.

Yet, for Frank Lampard, international football star and today very much his own man, there are so many other memories still to be created.

Frank Lampard has just got started.

Just watch for that dashing run, the confidence, the strength and potency and energy, the capability with that flash of toned and trained legs and the connection with the ball, probably some yards outside the penalty box.

We can call him the king of the King's Road...

Chapter Twenty-Eight

Joseph, Mary and Jose

'It would be unjust to Jose and the players to
say we've won this on the back of money. Every result
they've got, they've earned.'

CHELSEA CHIEF EXECUTIVE PETER KENYON, 23 APRIL 2005

In the final days of the Premiership and the Champions
League, Frank Lampard strode through like Chelsea's
guide to the trophies, an assured, commanding figure on
and off the pitch. One of today's most glorious performers
in sport, Frank belted in the second goal when Chelsea
triumphed over Fulham 3-1 in their London Derby on 23
April 2005. Indeed, the whole season seemed to have been
one long cavalcade of a coronation.

That Saturday, it was fifty years to the day since his team
had last won the Premiership and they were within one
result of repeating that achievement with their 26th win
in 34 League games. If Arsenal, in second place, failed to
defeat Spurs 48 hours later then the title was in the record
books. Although Arsène Wenger conceded that Chelsea
were 'very worthy' Premiership Champions, his team
denied them early official celebrations. Chelsea had

waited half a century – and they would have to wait a little longer.

Jose Mourinho knew that his team had no doubts of their stature and said after the Fulham game: 'They were magnificent and at the end they felt they deserved to be champions.'

Sir Alex Ferguson suggested it had been over for Manchester United from the start, from their first game at Stamford Bridge which they lost 1–0 on 15 August 2004, 'We never caught up with Chelsea since then.

'This season is the first I can remember where I have to look at the first game and say that was the the title decider.'

Months later, yes, the players did a lap of honour at Stamford Bridge after that Fulham encounter and given Chelsea's fourteen point lead, you had to be a rather anal statistician to resent that. All that was left was a rubber stamp, two points, and that was pretty certain away to Bolton Wanderers on 30 April. A long time since 23 April 1955, when they beat Sheffield Wednesday at home to win their only previous League title, and Roy Bentley was the captain. Roy Bentley was present, as guest of honour of the Blues, for the Fulham game and took a bow at half time.

There's a long legacy to Chelsea which Frank Lampard appreciates. He's grown up with football with all its beauty and its cruelty. In the dwindling days of the 2005 season at arguably the most golden moments in the club's history there was an extravagant excitement to being such a high-profile Chelsea star.

Yet he remained cool and calm – even after the monumental Champions League semi-final at home to

Liverpool. They had a red carpet rolled out down the tunnel at Stamford Bridge on that Wednesday evening, 27 April 2005; it was called the 'road to Istanbul', where one of the English clubs would meet AC Milan in the richly anticipated, phenomenal final. In what had been the biggest game of the English season Jose Mourinho had coached his team to play, ironically, not with a Continental passion but more of stiff upper lip. They kept in control enough not to concede an away goal. But neither did they score.

Frank, covered in praise for his heart-stopping performance at Bolton's Reebok stadium, completed his 4,570th minute of play, of solid game time, when Chelsea took the Premiership title with three matches to spare. It was Chelsea's 27th win in 35 League games since opening day and their defeat of Manchester United at Stamford Bridge. Frank starred in every game, his double at Bolton taking his goals for his most magnificent season to eighteen.

Commentators immediately singled out the English duo of Frank and John Terry as the basis for the glory. Yet Frank himself, elated at scoring the goals that sealed the title, said, 'This championship was not about a few individuals winning but the whole squad, management and backroom staff.'

The inspiration may have been Continental from superstar coach Jose Mourinho, the finances from Russia, but that reaction was the cool understatement of an Englishman.

The East End boy did good, very good indeed, up the West End.

Chapter Twenty-Nine
Lampard the Legend

'I have a Spanish girlfriend, a half-Spanish daughter
and a Portuguese manager. All the new experiences
have affected me in a good way.'

FRANK LAMPARD, NOVEMBER 2005

So good that, as World Cup fever heightened in 2006, he was being called Lampard the Legend.

Probably the most used phrase about Frank, as it was by Alan Shearer after the England–Argentina encounter in November 2005, was: 'He's a world-class player.' Certainly, his manager has no doubts. Jose Mourinho paid Frank an overwhelming tribute: 'He is a complete player. He is very strong in every aspect. I wouldn't swap him for any player: Ronaldinho, Kaka or Andrei Shevchenko. He plays every game if it rains or snows. Away or home, soft or difficult opponents, whether they play a zonal system against him or are aggressive. He is my perfect player and I wouldn't change him for anyone.'

But being perfect does have its handicaps. If you don't deliver perfection every time, then the doom watchers snarl that you've lost your touch. Also, in Frank's case, his expectations, as well as those of his fans, go forever skywards.

At the start of 2006, he had an astonishing year to look back on: he set a Premiership record on 26 November 2005, when he walked out against Portsmouth at Fratton Park for his 160th consecutive league appearance. His record-breaking run – 164 consecutive matches – ended when Chelsea beat Manchester City 1–0 (courtesy of a Joe Cole goal) on 28 December 2005. A virus stopped his incredible sequence just ten minutes before the start of the game. Jose Mourinho revealed Frank's determination to play: 'Frank was feeling bad during the day. He wanted to play but during the warm-up he realised it was impossible. It was a big test for the players to play without him. But the answer of the team was magnificent. People talk about the power of money but I don't agree. This is the power of a group, the power of a group of friends, human beings playing together.'

Yet Frank's consistency has set him apart from all others. His goal-scoring, readiness to fight injury and cool temperament make him the ultimate gladiator.

Frank tried to play down his achievement when it became apparent he would beat David James's total of 159 consecutive games. But Mourinho said that his 'perfect player' had had it in his sights for some time. With two games to go to the end of the season and Chelsea already champions, Lampard could have opted for early surgery on his toe. But he played on through the pain and reaped his accolades at Portsmouth. Mourinho said, 'He preferred to do it after games against Manchester United and Newcastle and carry on.'

LAMPARD THE LEGEND

Despite Frank's yeoman tendencies, his manager was not concerned about how much he would help England in the World Cup. A combination of occasional rest in less vital games and a month-long gap before the start of the tournament meant Frank would be on top of the game in Germany: 'He is a player who can recover well. He is very strong physically. Training with Chelsea is controlled and that means he can play a hard season in England.

'An intelligent manager can perfectly rest his players, start working again and prepare for a good World Cup, and Frank has, in Sven-Goran Eriksson, an experienced and intelligent person to control that. So I think also he will have a good World Cup.'

Yet, Frank is looking forward to a great tournament: he has never been one to rest on his laurels. And they are heavyweight.

At the end of 2005, he was voted second in the FIFA World Player of the Year poll, with only Ronaldinho considered above him; the same result was returned for the Ballon D'Or, Europe's top award. At the start of 2006, the England fans awarded him their Player of the Year trophy. Add the Premiership crown, Carling Cup, Football Writers' Player of the Year, a record for consecutive Premier League appearances and qualification for the World Cup as top scorer and you understand where Lampard the Legend came from. He played sixty-three games and scored twenty-eight goals in 2005. Always one for high standards, he thinks he should have done better. 'I want more. I need to get my head down and keep trying to improve. I was very pleased. I wouldn't say I can't believe it because I've always strived to get to the very top, but it was a fantastic year for the club and the biggest prize was for the team in winning the League.

'But to come second in the FIFA vote tops it off on a personal level. The team awards are the most important, but as personal ones go this is the highest you can get.

'England qualifying for the World Cup was a big thing for me. I didn't play in the last one and so to be a big part in getting us there and to know that we will be playing in the finals was a great end to the campaign for me.

'Winning the Football Writers' Player of the Year was fantastic recognition and a great night, as well as being second in the European awards.

'The one thing which rates above all of those, however, was the birth of my daughter Luna. Seeing her every morning – her smile – nothing on the football pitch can match that and it was the year's crowning moment for me.

'A baby gives you something extra in your life. It's a great change, the best change you can have, and it's nice to have a bit more perspective. Because of her, I don't come home and beat myself up after a bad game, as I would have done a few years ago.

'Football is an obsession. It's always in the back of your mind and, if I lived alone, I would probably sit around watching football on TV all the time. I always understood that there was more to life than football, but it's much easier when you come home to a little smiley face.'

Yet, even if he has his little girl Luna – Spanish for 'moon' – to be obsessed about as well as football, Lampard insisted that in 2006 the burning ambition of everyone at

Stamford Bridge was to become only the second team to win the Premiership in consecutive years. But there seems an understanding that Chelsea feel they must dominate English football in the way that Manchester United had, during their eight titles in the Premiership era, to convince people of their true greatness.

'We didn't set out to win one title and fade away. We set out not just to win back-to-back, but to win more and more in English football. You have to give ultimate respect to United, who managed to do that while Arsenal, despite their title successes, didn't. We will try very hard to win consecutive titles and we are hungry to go after that.

'Only when you have won one title and know what it takes can you understand better how great an achievement it was for United to win so many.

'We aspire to be what Liverpool were in the seventies and eighties and what Manchester United have been for the past ten years. That means not just winning the title two years on the trot, but doing it over the next five to ten years.

'In the second year, it is much harder because everyone lifts their performances against you and not only opposing players but also fans are more up for it.

'If anything goes wrong, people jump on it and say, "Is this the big blip?"

'There are a lot of things on and off the pitch that you have to be even stronger to cope with after you win the first championship, and United became the best at that. They had success for ten years, winning it back-to-back a few times. We are becoming accustomed to the demands more and more.

'Of course, I want to win the League but we want to win the Champions League and avenge the two semi-finals which we lost [to Monaco and Liverpool]. It sounds greedy to even talk about it, but yes I have aspirations to win them all.'

And that other big tournament?

'As for the World Cup, I believe in our team both individually and collectively. I think that we can go to Germany and do well. People talk about me being the most improved player and perhaps that is simply because I just want to get better, year after year.'

It's an acknowledged fact that no player in the English game has made more of their basic talents, no player shown greater determination to improve their game, their fitness, leadership skills and image. He's made a terrific personal journey from being a figure of some fun for West Ham fans to one of world football's greatest stars. And one of the most admired. He gave an astonishing performance when he was named Footballer of the Year by the Football Writers' Association. One guest pointed out, 'A speech was required. In the same situation, Eric Cantona once honoured us with thirty seconds. Lampard treated us to more like thirty minutes of graciousness and gratitude.

'He thanked all his old coaches, his family and friends who had helped him to this point. He treasured the award, he said, because it was not just about playing ability, but also about how a player carried and conducted himself.

'There was even humour. Gordon Strachan had earlier passed on a question from his wife to Lampard: "How did you get rid of that fat arse?"

'"Tell her to come back on the first day of pre-season training and she'll be able to see it again," he replied.'

Chapter Thirty
Captain Marvellous

'English football has found its conscience, its voice.'

PAUL HAYWARD, THE DAILY MAIL, 23 NOVEMBER 2005

Frank's work for the Teenage Cancer Trust, which he has done quietly but intently, has won him amazing admiration.

In November 2005, he was one of the hosts, together with Roger Daltrey of The Who and designer Karen Millen, of a fundraising evening at Old Billingsgate in London.

Frank worked the room like an Oscar nominee; there was time for everyone as he introduced his fiancée Elen Rives. He seemed nervous but happy to be there.

'Frank Lampard's Evening for Teenage Cancer Trust' followed his visit to see two teenage Chelsea fans, brothers both diagnosed with lymphoma. One died in July last year. A few weeks earlier, Frank took eleven-year-old Lucy Hilton on to the pitch when Chelsea were presented with the Premiership trophy. Her brain tumour killed her only a few days later.

The distinguished sports writer Paul Hayward said in the Daily Mail on 23 November 2005: 'There is not a famous person in Britain who could have loaded more compassion into a speech about this truly evil disease and how it steals life from the young.

'Lampard played one of the great games of his life. It came twenty-four hours after he had made his 159th consecutive Premiership appearance.

'Off the pitch and on it, this son of old East-End footballing stock has developed into a statesman, philanthropist and inspiration. Many of us went to Old Billingsgate on the banks of the Thames thinking John Terry is Chelsea's leading candidate to succeed David Beckham as England captain. We left acknowledging a more powerful truth about Lampard's ability to see beyond the white lines of a football field.

'No slight is intended against Terry, who cheekily bid £13,000 for a day at Arsenal's training ground and pressed the flesh all night. But, if either of them can teach young disciples of the game that you can be a caring member of society as well as a billboard god, then it's surely the man about to reach 160 not out.'

The Teenage Cancer Trust was, and is, raising funds for special units – each one costs £1.5 million – for young cancer sufferers. They look like the Big Brother house, have pool tables and cable television, and most importantly are making a 15 per cent difference to recovery rates. Eight exist and four more are on the way, but another ten are needed. The Trust said they were thrilled and proud to have Frank as one of their ambassadors.

He took no credit for helping raise more than half a million pounds at Old Billingsgate. However, he does take credit for Luna. Her fortunes seem entangled with England's World Cup hope. When he scored from the penalty spot to make it England 1 Austria 0, on 8 October 2005, he pointed skywards and exclaimed, 'That's for you, Luna!'

On 24 August that year, five days after Luna was born, Frank scored the opener (Chelsea 4 West Bromwich Albion 0), his 50th Chelsea goal, and a baby-rocking celebration followed. He dedicates all his goals to his little girl. He adores her. In former days, he would be 'over the moon' but now she's named after the satellite.

Elen Rives opted for a Caesarean birth. She particularly wanted her grandmother, 93, who was on holiday from Barcelona to see the baby, and Frank explained, 'It was planned around that rather than around football.'

Luna Coco Patricia (for Frank's mother) Lampard was born at the Portland Hospital in West London, where David and Victoria Beckham's sons Brooklyn and Romeo were born. She then returned to her parents' £8.4 million house in Chelsea and their French mastiff, Daphne. There the alarm on Frank's mobile is set for 8am, although Luna's usually woken him before that.

A couple of months after his daughter was born, Frank explained his daily routine: 'I'm sure things will get a lot earlier, a lot more hectic. Right now, I've got about three-quarters of an hour before I leave for training. I don't bother showering. I just freshen up, stick on jeans and trainers, let the dog out and get her food. Daphne's a

French mastiff – like the one in that movie Turner & Hooch. She slobbers a bit, but she's got a beautiful face.

'Breakfast is usually a mug of strong English-breakfast tea and a bowl of Coco Pops. If I get bored, the Frosties come out. But I always go back to Coco Pops – I've been having them since I was a kid.

'We get the Sun, Mirror and Daily Mail delivered, so I usually have a quick flick through and then set off in the car – a blue Aston Martin – for the training ground in Cobham. I'll turn on the radio or listen to music. I like U2 and Coldplay.

'There are days when it's harder to motivate yourself – you're tired or have things on your mind, but on the whole I enjoy it. I'm a bit of a fitness fanatic, anyway. I got that from my father.

'I wanted to be a footballer for as long as I can remember. It was all I thought about. But right from the start, Dad drummed it into me that as well as practice you had to be fit. Training lasts about an hour and a half, then it's in the shower and lunch.

'I eat at the ground, where they do things like pastas, salads, meat, chicken and fish. There's not much I don't like when it comes to food, and there aren't too many rules about what we should and shouldn't eat. But obviously, for extra energy, I tend to load up with more carbs a couple of days before a game. After lunch, I try to keep my days clear, so I can head back home to Elen and the baby. But I do a bit of charity work and I'm currently involved in the Tesco Sport for Schools and Clubs scheme, which is aimed at inspiring kids to take up a sport.

'I've already bought her first Chelsea outfit. I even got her a shirt with No. 8 on the back – the full works. When I got it, I didn't show Elen, I just rushed upstairs and put it on Luna. When I came down and Elen saw her, she said, "She's not going out of the house dressed like that!" I love singing nursery rhymes to Luna. The only thing is, I can't remember most of the words, so I have to make them up.

'In the afternoon, Mum often pops round for a cup of tea. Her and Dad have bought a place in London, which is great, and also means they're at all the games. I'm very close to Mum – a real mummy's boy, to be honest. We're very similar. Quite sensitive, quite shy. Whereas Dad's been the big influence on my career, Mum's been the one who shaped me as a person: you know, how to treat people, manners, that kind of thing. These days, she juggles a lot of her time between me and my two older sisters, as they've also got little girls.

'I'll usually take Daphne out for a walk or a run. Or sometimes I'll go out shopping. Occasionally, I'll have a blast – I bought a couple of lovely Yves Saint Laurent suits in Sloane Street, and a belt from Dolce & Gabbana. I'm not really into buying the latest gadgets, but I do appreciate something like a good watch.

'Sometimes we'll all drive out to a country village, maybe go looking for antiques – I love old furniture. We've only been in our house about six months, so we're still looking for things.

'Elen and I go out for a meal a couple of times a week, but we eat in the rest of the time. I've got a thing for M&S's chicken in breadcrumbs at the minute. So it'll be something like that with jacket potato and salad. Elen mainly does the cooking, but occasionally I'll throw a few bits together – maybe a pasta with tomato, chilli and garlic. Normally it comes out OK – not always.

'Then we might relax in front of the telly. I love things like The Sopranos and I confess to getting addicted to things like Big Brother and The X Factor. But, if it's something like Question Time, I just end up shouting at the box.

'Before bed I'll let the dog out, do the lights, the alarm and then I might read for a while.

'Sometimes, when I think about all those dreams I had as a kid and where I am now, I have to pinch myself.

'The hard work, the determination, the sacrifices – they all paid off. Life right now couldn't be sweeter.'

Of course, for the legend that is Super Frank Lampard, some World Cup silverware could certainly add a little sugar for him – and his millions of fans.

FRANK – THE STATISTICS

Real name	Frank Lampard
Height	6ft
Weight	13st 5lb
Date of birth	21 June 1978
Place of birth	Romford
Position	Midfielder
Nationality	English
International Caps	37
International Goals	10
Current Club	Chelsea
Signed on	14 June 2001
Fee	£ 11 million
Squad number	8

ALL-TIME PLAYING CAREER

Club	From	To	Fee	League		FA Cup		League Cup		Other	
Chelsea	14-06-01	Present	£11m	171(4)	47	18(3)	5	11(5)	2	37(2)	11
Swansea	06-10-95		Loan	8 (1)	1	0 (0)	0	0 (0)	0	1 (1)	0
West Ham	01-08-92	14-06-01	Trainee	132 (16)	24	13 (0)	2	15 (1)	9	10 (0)	4
Totals			£11m	311 (21)	72	31 (3)	7	26 (6)	11	48 (3)	15

GAMES PLAYED BY FRANK LAMPARD IN 1995–96

					Goals/Cards
05-05-1996	English Premier	West Ham	1–1	Sheff Wed	0

Goals: 0 Yellow cards: 0 Red Cards: 0

GAMES PLAYED BY FRANK LAMPARD IN 1996–97

					Goals/Cards
17-08-1996	English Premier	Arsenal	2–0	West Ham	0
04-09-1996	English Premier	Middlesbro	4–1	West Ham	0
18-09-1996	English League Cup	Barnet	1–1	West Ham	0
21-09-1996	English Premier	Nottm Forest	0–2	West Ham	0
26-10-1996	English Premier	West Ham	2–1	Blackburn	0
27-11-1996	English League Cup	West Ham	1–1	Stockport	0
30-11-1996	English Premier	Sheff Wed	0–0	West Ham	0
21-12-1996	English Premier	Chelsea	3–1	West Ham	0
28-12-1996	English Premier	West Ham	2–0	Sunderland	0

Date	Competition				Goals/Cards
01-01-1997	English Premier	West Ham	0–1	Nottm Forest	0
25-01-1997	English FA Cup	West Ham	0–1	Wrexham	0
29-01-1997	English Premier	West Ham	1–2	Arsenal	0
15-02-1997	English Premier	Derby	1–0	West Ham	0
01-03-1997	English Premier	Leeds	1–0	West Ham	0
12-03-1997	English Premier	West Ham	3–2	Chelsea	0
15-03-1997	English Premier	Aston Villa	0–0	West Ham	0 Yellow Card

Goals: 0 Yellow cards: 1 Red Cards: 0

GAMES PLAYED BY FRANK LAMPARD IN 1997–98

Date	Competition				Goals/Cards
09-08-1997	English Premier	Barnsley	1–2	West Ham	1
13-08-1997	English Premier	West Ham	2–1	Tottenham	0
23-08-1997	English Premier	Everton	2–1	West Ham	0
13-09-1997	English Premier	Man Utd	2–1	West Ham	0
16-09-1997	English League Cup	Huddersfield	1–0	West Ham	0

Date	Competition	Home	Score	Away	Goals	Card
20-09-1997	English Premier	West Ham	0–1	Newcastle	0	
24-09-1997	English Premier	Arsenal	4–0	West Ham	0	Yellow Card
27-09-1997	English Premier	West Ham	2–1	Liverpool	0	
29-09-1997	English League Cup	West Ham	3–0	Huddersfield	0	
15-10-1997	English League Cup	West Ham	3–0	Aston Villa	1	
18-10-1997	English Premier	West Ham	3–0	Bolton	0	Yellow Card
27-10-1997	English Premier	Leicester	2–1	West Ham	0	
09-11-1997	English Premier	Chelsea	2–1	West Ham	0	
19-11-1997	English League Cup	West Ham	4–1	Walsall	3	
23-11-1997	English Premier	Leeds	3–1	West Ham	1	
06-12-1997	English Premier	Derby	2–0	West Ham	0	
13-12-1997	English Premier	West Ham	1–0	Sheff Wed	0	
20-12-1997	English Premier	Blackburn	3–0	West Ham	0	
26-12-1997	English Premier	West Ham	1–0	Coventry	0	Yellow Card
28-12-1997	English Premier	Milton Keynes	1–2	West Ham	0	
03-01-1998	English FA Cup	West Ham	2–1	W & Emley	1	
06-01-1998	English League Cup	West Ham	1–2	Arsenal	0	

10-01-1998	English Premier	West Ham	6–0	Barnsley	1
17-01-1998	English Premier	Tottenham	1–0	West Ham	0
25-01-1998	English FA Cup	Man City	1–2	West Ham	0
31-01-1998	English Premier	West Ham	2–2	Everton	0
14-02-1998	English FA Cup	West Ham	2–2	Blackburn	0
21-02-1998	English Premier	Bolton	1–1	West Ham	0
25-02-1998	English FA Cup	Blackburn	1–1	West Ham	0
02-03-1998	English Premier	West Ham	0–0	Arsenal	0
08-03-1998	English FA Cup	Arsenal	1–1	West Ham	0 Yellow Card
11-03-1998	English Premier	West Ham	1–1	Man Utd	0 Yellow Card
14-03-1998	English Premier	West Ham	2–1	Chelsea	0
17-03-1998	English FA Cup	West Ham	1–1	Arsenal	0
04-04-1998	English Premier	Aston Villa	2–0	West Ham	0
11-04-1998	English Premier	West Ham	0–0	Derby	0
13-04-1998	English Premier	Sheff Wed	1–1	West Ham	0
18-04-1998	English Premier	West Ham	2–1	Blackburn	0
25-04-1998	English Premier	West Ham	2–4	Southampton	0

02-05-1998	English Premier	Liverpool	5–0	West Ham	0
05-05-1998	English Premier	C Palace	3–3	West Ham	0 Yellow Card
10-05-1998	English Premier	West Ham	4–3	Leicester	1

Goals: 9 Yellow Cards: 6 Red Cards: 0

GAMES PLAYED BY FRANK LAMPARD IN 1998–99

					Goals/Cards
15-08-1998	English Premier	Sheff Wed	0–1	West Ham	0 Yellow Card
22-08-1998	English Premier	West Ham	0–0	Man Utd	0
29-08-1998	English Premier	Coventry	0–0	West Ham	0
09-09-1998	English Premier	West Ham	3–4	Milton Keynes	0
12-09-1998	English Premier	West Ham	2–1	Liverpool	0
15-09-1998	English League Cup	Northampton	2–0	West Ham	0
19-09-1998	English Premier	Nottm Forest	0–0	West Ham	0
22-09-1998	English League Cup	West Ham	1–0	Northampton	1
28-09-1998	English Premier	West Ham	1–0	Southampton	0

Date	Competition	Score			Yellow Card
03-10-1998	English Premier	3–0	Blackburn	West Ham	0
17-10-1998	English Premier	0–0	West Ham	Aston Villa	0
24-10-1998	English Premier	4–2	Charlton	West Ham	0
31-10-1998	English Premier	0–3	Newcastle	West Ham	0
08-11-1998	English Premier	1–1	West Ham	Chelsea	0
14-11-1998	English Premier	3–2	West Ham	Leicester	1
22-11-1998	English Premier	0–2	Derby	West Ham	0
28-11-1998	English Premier	2–1	West Ham	Tottenham	0
05-12-1998	English Premier	4–0	Leeds	West Ham	0
12-12-1998	English Premier	1–0	Middlesbro	West Ham	0
19-12-1998	English Premier	2–1	West Ham	Everton	0
26-12-1998	English Premier	1–0	Arsenal	West Ham	0
28-12-1998	English Premier	2–0	West Ham	Coventry	0
10-01-1999	English Premier	4–1	Man Utd	West Ham	1
13-01-1999	English FA Cup	1–0	Swansea	West Ham	0
16-01-1999	English Premier	0–4	West Ham	Sheff Wed	0
30-01-1999	English Premier	0–0	Milton Keynes	West Ham	0

FRANK STATISTICS

06-02-1999	English Premier	West Ham	0-4	Arsenal	0
13-02-1999	English Premier	West Ham	2-1	Nottm Forest	1
20-02-1999	English Premier	Liverpool	2-2	West Ham	1
27-02-1999	English Premier	West Ham	2-0	Blackburn	0
06-03-1999	English Premier	Southampton	1-0	West Ham	0
13-03-1999	English Premier	Chelsea	0-1	West Ham	0
20-03-1999	English Premier	West Ham	2-0	Newcastle	0
02-04-1999	English Premier	Aston Villa	0-0	West Ham	0
05-04-1999	English Premier	West Ham	0-1	Charlton	0
10-04-1999	English Premier	Leicester	0-0	West Ham	0
17-04-1999	English Premier	West Ham	5-1	Derby	0
24-04-1999	English Premier	Tottenham	1-2	West Ham	0
01-05-1999	English Premier	West Ham	1-5	Leeds	0
08-05-1999	English Premier	Everton	6-0	West Ham	0
16-05-1999	English Premier	West Ham	4-0	Middlesbro	1 Yellow Card

Goals: 6 Yellow Cards: 3 Red Cards: 0

GAMES PLAYED BY FRANK LAMPARD IN 1999–2000

					Goals/Cards
17-07-1999	UEFA Intertoto Cup	West Ham	1–0	FC Jokerit	0
24-07-1999	UEFA Intertoto Cup	FC Jokerit	1–1	West Ham	1
28-07-1999	UEFA Intertoto Cup	West Ham	1–0	Heerenveen	1
04-08-1999	UEFA Intertoto Cup	Heerenveen	0–1	West Ham	0
07-08-1999	English Premier	West Ham	1–0	Tottenham	1
10-08-1999	UEFA Intertoto Cup	West Ham	0–1	Metz	0 Yellow Card
16-08-1999	English Premier	Aston Villa	2–2	West Ham	0 Yellow Card
21-08-1999	English Premier	West Ham	2–1	Leicester	0
24-08-1999	UEFA Intertoto Cup	Metz	1–3	West Ham	1
28-08-1999	English Premier	Bradford	0–3	West Ham	0
11-09-1999	English Premier	West Ham	1–0	Watford	0
16-09-1999	UEFA Cup	West Ham	3–0	Osijek	1
19-09-1999	English Premier	Everton	1–0	West Ham	0 Yellow Card
25-09-1999	English Premier	Coventry	1–0	West Ham	0
30-09-1999	UEFA Cup	Osijek	1–3	West Ham	0

03-10-1999	English Premier	West Ham	2-1	Arsenal	0
10-10-1999	International	England	2-1	Belgium	0
13-10-1999	English League Cup	West Ham	2-0	Bournemouth	1
17-10-1999	English Premier	Middlesbro	2-0	West Ham	0
21-10-1999	UEFA Cup	Steaua Bucharest	2-0	West Ham	0
24-10-1999	English Premier	West Ham	1-1	Sunderland	0
27-10-1999	English Premier	Liverpool	1-0	West Ham	0
30-10-1999	English Premier	Leeds	1-0	West Ham	0
04-11-1999	UEFA Cup	West Ham	0-0	Steaua Bucharest	0
07-11-1999	English Premier	Chelsea	0-0	West Ham	0
21-11-1999	English Premier	West Ham	4-3	Sheff Wed	1
27-11-1999	English Premier	West Ham	1-0	Liverpool	0
30-11-1999	English League Cup	Birmingham	2-3	West Ham	0
06-12-1999	English Premier	Tottenham	0-0	West Ham	0
11-12-1999	English FA Cup	Tranmere	1-0	West Ham	0
15-12-1999	English League Cup	West Ham	2-2	Aston Villa	1
18-12-1999	English Premier	West Ham	2-4	Man Utd	0

Date	Competition	Home	Score	Away	Goals	Cards
26-12-1999	English Premier	Milton Keynes	2–2	West Ham	0	1 Yellow Card
28-12-1999	English Premier	West Ham	1–1	Derby	0	0
03-01-2000	English Premier	Newcastle	2–2	West Ham	1	1
11-01-2000	English League Cup	West Ham	1–3	Aston Villa	1	1 Yellow Card
15-01-2000	English Premier	West Ham	1–1	Aston Villa	0	0
22-01-2000	English Premier	Leicester	1–3	West Ham	0	0
05-02-2000	English Premier	Southampton	2–1	West Ham	1	1
12-02-2000	English Premier	West Ham	5–4	Bradford	1	1 Yellow Card
04-03-2000	English Premier	Watford	1–2	West Ham	0	0
08-03-2000	English Premier	West Ham	2–0	Southampton	0	0
11-03-2000	English Premier	Sheff Wed	3–1	West Ham	1	1
18-03-2000	English Premier	West Ham	0–0	Chelsea	0	0
26-03-2000	English Premier	West Ham	2–1	Milton Keynes	0	0
01-04-2000	English Premier	Man Utd	7–1	West Ham	0	0
12-04-2000	English Premier	West Ham	2–1	Newcastle	0	0
15-04-2000	English Premier	Derby	1–2	West Ham	0	0
22-04-2000	English Premier	West Ham	5–0	Coventry	0	0

FRANK STATISTICS

| 29-04-2000 | English Premier | West Ham | 0-1 | Middlesbro | 0 |

Goals: 0 Yellow Cards: 1 Red Cards: 0

GAMES PLAYED BY FRANK LAMPARD IN 2000-01

					Goals/Cards
19-08-2000	English Premier	Chelsea	4-2	West Ham	0 Yellow Card
05-09-2000	English Premier	Sunderland	1-1	West Ham	0
11-09-2000	English Premier	Tottenham	1-0	West Ham	0 Yellow Card
23-09-2000	English Premier	Coventry	0-3	West Ham	1
27-09-2000	English League Cup	West Ham	1-1	Walsall	0
14-10-2000	English Premier	Ipswich	1-1	West Ham	0
21-10-2000	English Premier	West Ham	1-2	Arsenal	0
28-10-2000	English Premier	West Ham	1-0	Newcastle	0
31-10-2000	English League Cup	West Ham	2-0	Blackburn	0
06-11-2000	English Premier	Derby	0-0	West Ham	0
11-11-2000	English Premier	West Ham	4-1	Man City	0

18-11-2000	English Premier	Leeds	0-1	West Ham	0
25-11-2000	English Premier	Southampton	2-3	West Ham	0
29-11-2000	English League Cup	West Ham	1-2	Sheff Wed	1
02-12-2000	English Premier	West Ham	1-0	Middlesbro	0
16-12-2000	English Premier	Everton	1-1	West Ham	0
23-12-2000	English Premier	Leicester	2-1	West Ham	0
26-12-2000	English Premier	West Ham	5-0	Charlton	1
01-01-2001	English Premier	Man Utd	3-1	West Ham	0
06-01-2001	English FA Cup	Walsall	2-3	West Ham	1
13-01-2001	English Premier	West Ham	0-2	Sunderland	0
22-01-2001	English Premier	Charlton	1-1	West Ham	0
28-01-2001	English FA Cup	Man Utd	0-1	West Ham	0
31-01-2001	English Premier	West Ham	0-0	Tottenham	0
03-02-2001	English Premier	Liverpool	3-0	West Ham	0
12-02-2001	English Premier	West Ham	1-1	Coventry	0
17-02-2001	English FA Cup	Sunderland	0-1	West Ham	0
24-02-2001	English Premier	Bradford	1-2	West Ham	2

FRANK STATISTICS

Date	Competition	Team	Score	Opponent	Goals/Cards
28-02-2001	International	England	3–0	Spain	0
03-03-2001	English Premier	Arsenal	3–0	West Ham	0
07-03-2001	English Premier	West Ham	0–2	Chelsea	0
11-03-2001	English FA Cup	West Ham	2–3	Tottenham	0
17-03-2001	English Premier	West Ham	0–1	Ipswich	0 Yellow Card
31-03-2001	English Premier	West Ham	0–2	Everton	0
07-04-2001	English Premier	Aston Villa	2–2	West Ham	1
14-04-2001	English Premier	West Ham	3–1	Derby	1
16-04-2001	English Premier	Newcastle	2–1	West Ham	1
21-04-2001	English Premier	West Ham	0–2	Leeds	0

Goals: 9 Yellow Cards: 3 Red Cards: 0

GAMES PLAYED BY FRANK LAMPARD IN 2001–02

Date	Competition	Team	Score	Opponent	Goals/Cards
15-08-2001	International	England	0–2	Holland	0
19-08-2001	English Premier	Chelsea	1–1	Newcastle	0

25-08-2001	English Premier	Southampton	0–2	Chelsea	0
08-09-2001	English Premier	Chelsea	1–1	Arsenal	0
16-09-2001	English Premier	Tottenham	2–3	Chelsea	0 Red Card
20-09-2001	UEFA Cup	Chelsea	3–0	Levski Sofia	1
23-09-2001	English Premier	Chelsea	2–2	Middlesbro	0
27-09-2001	UEFA Cup	Levski Sofia	0–2	Chelsea	0
13-10-2001	English Premier	Chelsea	2–0	Leicester	0
18-10-2001	UEFA Cup	Hapoel Tel Aviv	2–0	Chelsea	0
21-10-2001	English Premier	Leeds	0–0	Chelsea	0
24-10-2001	English Premier	West Ham	2–1	Chelsea	0
28-10-2001	English Premier	Derby	1–1	Chelsea	0
01-11-2001	UEFA Cup	Chelsea	1–1	Hapoel Tel Aviv	0
04-11-2001	English Premier	Chelsea	2–1	Ipswich	0
10-11-2001	International	England	1–1	Sweden	0
18-11-2001	English Premier	Everton	0–0	Chelsea	0
24-11-2001	English Premier	Chelsea	0–0	Blackburn	0
28-11-2001	English League Cup	Leeds	0–2	Chelsea	0

FRANK STATISTICS

Date	Competition	Home	Score	Away	Yellow Card
01-12-2001	English Premier	Man Utd	0–3	Chelsea	0
05-12-2001	English Premier	Chelsea	0–1	Charlton	0
09-12-2001	English Premier	Sunderland	0–0	Chelsea	0
12-12-2001	English League Cup	Chelsea	1–0	Newcastle	0
16-12-2001	English Premier	Chelsea	4–0	Liverpool	0
23-12-2001	English Premier	Chelsea	5–1	Bolton	1
26-12-2001	English Premier	Arsenal	2–1	Chelsea	1
29-12-2001	English Premier	Newcastle	1–2	Chelsea	0
01-01-2002	English Premier	Chelsea	2–4	Southampton	0
05-01-2002	English FA Cup	Norwich	0–0	Chelsea	0
09-01-2002	English League Cup	Chelsea	2–1	Tottenham	0
12-01-2002	English Premier	Bolton	2–2	Chelsea	0
16-01-2002	English FA Cup	Chelsea	4–0	Norwich	1
20-01-2002	English Premier	Chelsea	5–1	West Ham	0
23-01-2002	English League Cup	Tottenham	5–1	Chelsea	0
26-01-2002	English FA Cup	Chelsea	1–1	West Ham	0
30-01-2002	English Premier	Chelsea	2–0	Leeds	0

Date	Competition	Team	Score	Opponent	
02-02-2002	English Premier	Leicester	2–3	Chelsea	0
06-02-2002	English FA Cup	West Ham	2–3	Chelsea	0
09-02-2002	English Premier	Aston Villa	1–1	Chelsea	1
13-02-2002	International	Holland	1–1	England	0
17-02-2002	English FA Cup	Chelsea	3–1	Preston	0
02-03-2002	English Premier	Charlton	2–1	Chelsea	1 Yellow Card
06-03-2002	English Premier	Chelsea	3–2	Fulham	0
10-03-2002	English FA Cup	Tottenham	0–4	Chelsea	0
13-03-2002	English Premier	Chelsea	4–0	Tottenham	1
16-03-2002	English Premier	Chelsea	4–0	Sunderland	0
24-03-2002	English Premier	Liverpool	1–0	Chelsea	0
27-03-2002	International	England	1–2	Italy	0
30-03-2002	English Premier	Chelsea	2–1	Derby	0 Yellow Card
01-04-2002	English Premier	Ipswich	0–0	Chelsea	0
06-04-2002	English Premier	Chelsea	3–0	Everton	0
10-04-2002	English Premier	Blackburn	0–0	Chelsea	0
14-04-2002	English FA Cup	Fulham	0–1	Chelsea	0

17-04-2002	International	England	4-0	Paraguay	0
20-04-2002	English Premier	Chelsea	0-3	Man Utd	0
27-04-2002	English Premier	Middlesbro	0-2	Chelsea	0
04-05-2002	English FA Cup	Arsenal	2-0	Chelsea	0
11-05-2002	English Premier	Chelsea	1-3	Aston Villa	0

Goals: 7 Yellow Cards: 3 Red Cards: 1

GAMES PLAYED BY FRANK LAMPARD IN 2002–03

					Goals/Cards
17-08-2002	English Premier	Charlton	2-3	Chelsea	1
23-08-2002	English Premier	Chelsea	2-2	Man Utd	0
28-08-2002	English Premier	Southampton	1-1	Chelsea	1
01-09-2002	English Premier	Chelsea	1-1	Arsenal	0 Yellow Card
11-09-2002	English Premier	Blackburn	2-3	Chelsea	0
14-09-2002	English Premier	Chelsea	3-0	Newcastle	0

Date	Competition	Team	Score	Opponent	Goals	
19-09-2002	UEFA Cup	Chelsea	2-1	Viking	0	
23-09-2002	English Premier	Fulham	0-0	Chelsea	0	
28-09-2002	English Premier	Chelsea	2-3	West Ham	0	
03-10-2002	UEFA Cup	Viking	4-2	Chelsea	1	
06-10-2002	English Premier	Liverpool	1-0	Chelsea	0	
19-10-2002	English Premier	Man City	0-3	Chelsea	0	Yellow Card
26-10-2002	English Premier	Chelsea	2-0	West Brom	0	
03-11-2002	English Premier	Tottenham	0-0	Chelsea	0	
06-11-2002	English League Cup	Chelsea	2-1	Gillingham	0	
09-11-2002	English Premier	Chelsea	3-0	Birmingham	0	
16-11-2002	English Premier	Chelsea	1-0	Middlesbro	0	
23-11-2002	English Premier	Bolton	1-1	Chelsea	0	
30-11-2002	English Premier	Chelsea	3-0	Sunderland	0	
04-12-2002	English League Cup	Chelsea	4-1	Everton	0	
07-12-2002	English Premier	Everton	1-3	Chelsea	0	Yellow Card
14-12-2002	English Premier	Middlesbro	1-1	Chelsea	0	
17-12-2002	English League Cup	Man Utd	1-0	Chelsea	0	

21-12-2002	English Premier	Chelsea	2–0	Aston Villa	1
26-12-2002	English Premier	Chelsea	0–0	Southampton	0
28-12-2002	English Premier	Leeds	2–0	Chelsea	0
01-01-2003	English Premier	Arsenal	3–2	Chelsea	0
04-01-2003	English FA Cup	Chelsea	1–0	Middlesbro	0
11-01-2003	English Premier	Chelsea	4–1	Charlton	0
18-01-2003	English Premier	Man Utd	2–1	Chelsea	0
26-01-2003	English FA Cup	Shrewsbury	0–4	Chelsea	0
28-01-2003	English Premier	Chelsea	3–2	Leeds	1
01-02-2003	English Premier	Chelsea	1–1	Tottenham	0
08-02-2003	English Premier	Birmingham	1–3	Chelsea	0
12-02-2003	International	England	1–3	Australia	0
16-02-2003	English FA Cup	Stoke	0–2	Chelsea	0
22-02-2003	English Premier	Chelsea	1–2	Blackburn	0
01-03-2003	English Premier	Newcastle	2–1	Chelsea	1
08-03-2003	English FA Cup	Arsenal	2–2	Chelsea	1
16-03-2003	English Premier	West Brom	0–2	Chelsea	0

Date	Competition	Home	Score	Away	
22-03-2003	English Premier	Chelsea	5–0	Man City	1
25-03-2003	English FA Cup	Chelsea	1–3	Arsenal	0
05-04-2003	English Premier	Sunderland	1–2	Chelsea	0
12-04-2003	English Premier	Chelsea	1–0	Bolton	0
19-04-2003	English Premier	Aston Villa	2–1	Chelsea	0
21-04-2003	English Premier	Chelsea	4–1	Everton	0
26-04-2003	English Premier	Chelsea	1–1	Fulham	0
03-05-2003	English Premier	West Ham	1–0	Chelsea	0
11-05-2003	English Premier	Chelsea	2–1	Liverpool	0
22-05-2003	International	South Africa	1–2	England	0
03-06-2003	International	England	2–1	Serbia & M	0
11-06-2003	European Championships	England	2–1	Slovakia	0

Goals: 8 Yellow Cards: 3 Red Cards: 0

FRANK STATISTICS

GAMES PLAYED BY FRANK LAMPARD IN 2003–04

Date	Competition	Opponent	Score		Goals/Cards
13-08-2003	European Cup	Zilina	0–2	Chelsea	0
17-08-2003	English Premier	Liverpool	1–2	Chelsea	0 Yellow Card
20-08-2003	International	England	3–1	Croatia	1
23-08-2003	English Premier	Chelsea	2–1	Leicester	0
26-08-2003	European Cup	Chelsea	3–0	Zilina	0
30-08-2003	English Premier	Chelsea	2–2	Blackburn	0
06-09-2003	European Championships	Macedonia	1–2	England	0
10-09-2003	European Championships	England	2–0	Liechtenstein	0
13-09-2003	English Premier	Chelsea	4–2	Tottenham	1
16-09-2003	European Cup	Sparta Prague	0–1	Chelsea	0
20-09-2003	English Premier	Wolves	0–5	Chelsea	1
27-09-2003	English Premier	Chelsea	1–0	Aston Villa	0
01-10-2003	European Cup	Chelsea	0–2	Besiktas	0

Date	Competition	Home	Score	Away	Notes
05-10-2003	English Premier	Middlesbro	1–2	Chelsea	0
11-10-2003	European Championships	Turkey	0–0	England	0
14-10-2003	English Premier	Birmingham	0–0	Chelsea	0
18-10-2003	English Premier	Arsenal	2–1	Chelsea	0
22-10-2003	European Cup	Chelsea	2–1	Lazio	1
25-10-2003	English Premier	Chelsea	1–0	Man City	0
01-11-2003	English Premier	Everton	0–1	Chelsea	0
04-11-2003	European Cup	Lazio	0–4	Chelsea	1
09-11-2003	English Premier	Chelsea	5–0	Newcastle	1
16-11-2003	International	England	2–3	Denmark	0
22-11-2003	English Premier	Southampton	0–1	Chelsea	0
26-11-2003	European Cup	Chelsea	0–0	Sparta Prague	0
30-11-2003	English Premier	Chelsea	1–0	Man Utd	1 Yellow Card
03-12-2003	English League Cup	Reading	0–1	Chelsea	0
06-12-2003	English Premier	Leeds	1–1	Chelsea	0
09-12-2003	European Cup	Besiktas	0–2	Chelsea	0

FRANK STATISTICS

Date	Competition	Team	Score	Opponent	Yellow Card
13-12-2003	English Premier	Chelsea	1–2	Bolton	0
17-12-2003	English League Cup	Aston Villa	2–1	Chelsea	0
20-12-2003	English Premier	Fulham	0–1	Chelsea	0
26-12-2003	English Premier	Charlton	4–2	Chelsea	0
28-12-2003	English Premier	Chelsea	3–0	Portsmouth	1
03-01-2004	English FA Cup	Watford	2–2	Chelsea	1
07-01-2004	English Premier	Chelsea	0–1	Liverpool	0
11-01-2004	English Premier	Leicester	0–4	Chelsea	0
14-01-2004	English FA Cup	Chelsea	4–0	Watford	0
18-01-2004	English Premier	Chelsea	0–0	Birmingham	0
24-01-2004	English FA Cup	Scarborough	0–1	Chelsea	0
01-02-2004	English Premier	Blackburn	2–3	Chelsea	2
08-02-2004	English Premier	Chelsea	1–0	Charlton	0
11-02-2004	English Premier	Portsmouth	0–2	Chelsea	0
15-02-2004	English FA Cup	Arsenal	2–1	Chelsea	0
18-02-2004	International	Portugal	1–1	England	0
21-02-2004	English Premier	Chelsea	1–2	Arsenal	0

Date	Competition	Home	Score	Away	Yellow Card
25-02-2004	European Cup	VfB Stuttgart	0-1	Chelsea	0
28-02-2004	English Premier	Man City	0-1	Chelsea	0
09-03-2004	European Cup	Chelsea	0-0	VfB Stuttgart	0
13-03-2004	English Premier	Bolton	0-2	Chelsea	0
20-03-2004	English Premier	Chelsea	2-1	Fulham	0
24-03-2004	European Cup	Chelsea	1-1	Arsenal	0
27-03-2004	English Premier	Chelsea	5-2	Wolves	1
03-04-2004	English Premier	Tottenham	0-1	Chelsea	0
06-04-2004	European Cup	Arsenal	1-2	Chelsea	1
10-04-2004	English Premier	Chelsea	0-0	Middlesbro	0
12-04-2004	English Premier	Aston Villa	3-2	Chelsea	0
17-04-2004	English Premier	Chelsea	0-0	Everton	0
20-04-2004	European Cup	Monaco	3-1	Chelsea	0
25-04-2004	English Premier	Newcastle	2-1	Chelsea	0
01-05-2004	English Premier	Chelsea	4-0	Southampton	2
05-05-2004	European Cup	Chelsea	2-2	Monaco	1
08-05-2004	English Premier	Man Utd	1-1	Chelsea	0

Date	Competition	Opponent	Score		Cards
15-05-2004	English Premier	Chelsea	1–0	Leeds	0
01-06-2004	International	England	1–1	Japan	0
05-06-2004	International	England	6–1	Iceland	1
13-06-2004	European Championships	France	2–1	England	1 Yellow Card
17-06-2004	European Championships	England	3–0	Switzerland	0
21-06-2004	European Championships	Croatia	2–4	England	1
24-06-2004	European Championships	Portugal	2–2	England	1

Goals: 19 Yellow Cards: 0 Red Cards: 0

GAMES PLAYED BY FRANK LAMPARD IN 2004–05

Date	Competition		Score		Goals/Cards
15-08-2004	English Premier	Chelsea	1–0	Man Utd	0
18-08-2004	International	England	3–0	Ukraine	0
21-08-2004	English Premier	Birmingham	0–1	Chelsea	0
24-08-2004	English Premier	C Palace	0–2	Chelsea	0
28-08-2004	English Premier	Chelsea	2–1	Southampton	1
04-09-2004	World Cup	Austria	2–2	England	1
08-09-2004	World Cup	Poland	1–2	England	0
11-09-2004	English Premier	Aston Villa	0–0	Chelsea	0
14-09-2004	European Cup	Paris St-G.	0–3	Chelsea	0 Yellow Card
19-09-2004	English Premier	Chelsea	0–0	Tottenham	0
25-09-2004	English Premier	Middlesbro	0–1	Chelsea	0
29-09-2004	European Cup	Chelsea	3–1	Porto	0
03-10-2004	English Premier	Chelsea	1–0	Liverpool	0
09-10-2004	World Cup	England	2–0	Wales	1
13-10-2004	World Cup	Azerbaijan	0–1	England	0

Date	Competition		Score		Yellow Card
16-10-2004	English Premier	Man City	1-0	Chelsea	0 Yellow Card
20-10-2004	European Cup	Chelsea	2-0	CSKA Moscow	0
23-10-2004	English Premier	Chelsea	4-0	Blackburn	0
27-10-2004	English League Cup	Chelsea	1-0	West Ham	0
30-10-2004	English Premier	West Brom	1-4	Chelsea	1
02-11-2004	European Cup	CSKA Moscow	0-1	Chelsea	0
06-11-2004	English Premier	Chelsea	1-0	Everton	0
10-11-2004	English League Cup	Newcastle	0-2	Chelsea	0
13-11-2004	English Premier	Fulham	1-4	Chelsea	1 Yellow Card
17-11-2004	International	Spain	1-0	England	0
20-11-2004	English Premier	Chelsea	2-2	Bolton	0
24-11-2004	European Cup	Chelsea	0-0	Paris St-G.	0
27-11-2004	English Premier	Charlton	0-4	Chelsea	0
30-11-2004	English League Cup	Fulham	1-2	Chelsea	1
04-12-2004	English Premier	Chelsea	4-0	Newcastle	1
07-12-2004	European Cup	Porto	2-1	Chelsea	0
12-12-2004	English Premier	Arsenal	2-2	Chelsea	0 Yellow Card

Date	Competition	Home	Score	Away	Goals	Card
18-12-2004	English Premier	Chelsea	4-0	Norwich	1	
26-12-2004	English Premier	Chelsea	1-0	Aston Villa	0	
28-12-2004	English Premier	Portsmouth	0-2	Chelsea	0	Yellow Card
01-01-2005	English Premier	Liverpool	0-1	Chelsea	0	Yellow Card
04-01-2005	English Premier	Chelsea	2-0	Middlesbro	0	
12-01-2005	English League Cup	Chelsea	0-0	Man Utd	0	
15-01-2005	English Premier	Tottenham	0-2	Chelsea	2	
22-01-2005	English Premier	Chelsea	3-0	Portsmouth	0	
26-01-2005	English League Cup	Man Utd	1-2	Chelsea	1	
30-01-2005	English FA Cup	Chelsea	2-0	Birmingham	0	
02-02-2005	English Premier	Blackburn	0-1	Chelsea	0	
06-02-2005	English Premier	Chelsea	0-0	Man City	0	
09-02-2005	International	England	0-0	Holland	0	
12-02-2005	English Premier	Everton	0-1	Chelsea	0	
20-02-2005	English FA Cup	Newcastle	1-0	Chelsea	0	
23-02-2005	European Cup	Barcelona	2-1	Chelsea	0	
27-02-2005	English League Cup	Liverpool	2-3	Chelsea	0	Yellow Card

FRANK STATISTICS

Date	Competition	Home	Score	Away	Yellow Card
05-03-2005	English Premier	Norwich	1-3	Chelsea	0
08-03-2005	European Cup	Chelsea	4-2	Barcelona	1
15-03-2005	English Premier	Chelsea	1-0	West Brom	0
19-03-2005	English Premier	Chelsea	4-1	C Palace	1
26-03-2005	World Cup	England	4-0	N Ireland	1
30-03-2005	World Cup	England	2-0	Azerbaijan	0
02-04-2005	English Premier	Southampton	1-3	Chelsea	1
06-04-2005	European Cup	Chelsea	4-2	B. Munich	2
09-04-2005	English Premier	Chelsea	1-1	Birmingham	0
12-04-2005	European Cup	B. Munich	3-2	Chelsea	1
20-04-2005	English Premier	Chelsea	0-0	Arsenal	0
23-04-2005	English Premier	Chelsea	3-1	Fulham	1
27-04-2005	European Cup	Chelsea	0-0	Liverpool	0
30-04-2005	English Premier	Bolton	0-2	Chelsea	2
03-05-2005	European Cup	Liverpool	1-0	Chelsea	0
07-05-2005	English Premier	Chelsea	1-0	Charlton	0
10-05-2005	English Premier	Man Utd	1-3	Chelsea	0

				Goals/Cards	
15-05-2005	English Premier	Newcastle	1–1	Chelsea	1	0 Yellow Card

GAMES PLAYED BY FRANK LAMPARD IN 2005–06

Date	Competition	Home	Score	Away	Goals/Cards	Yellow Card
07-08-2005	FA Community Shield	Chelsea	2–1	Arsenal	0	
14-08-2005	English Premier	Wigan	0–1	Chelsea	0	
17-08-2005	International	Denmark	4–1	England	0	
21-08-2005	English Premier	Chelsea	1–0	Arsenal	0	
24-08-2005	English Premier	Chelsea	4–0	West Brom	2	
27-08-2005	English Premier	Tottenham	0–2	Chelsea	0	
03-09-2005	World Cup	Wales	0–1	England	0	
07-09-2005	World Cup	Northern Ireland	1–0	England	0	
10-09-2005	English Premier	Chelsea	2–0	Sunderland	0	
13-09-2005	European Cup	Chelsea	1–0	Anderlecht	1	
17-09-2005	English Premier	Charlton	0–2	Chelsea	0	
24-09-2005	English Premier	Chelsea	2–1	Aston Villa	2	

FRANK STATISTICS

Date	Competition	Team	Score	Opponent	Cards
28-09-2005	European Cup	Liverpool	0–0	Chelsea	0 Yellow Card
02-10-2005	English Premier	Liverpool	1–4	Chelsea	1 Yellow Card
08-10-2005	World Cup	England	1–0	Austria	1
12-10-2005	World Cup	England	2–1	Poland	1
15-10-2005	English Premier	Chelsea	5–1	Bolton	2
19-10-2005	European Cup	Chelsea	4–0	Real Betis	0
23-10-2005	English Premier	Everton	1–1	Chelsea	1
26-10-2005	English League Cup	Chelsea	1–1	Charlton	0
29-10-2005	English Premier	Chelsea	4–2	Blackburn	2
01-11-2005	European Cup	Real Betis	1–0	Chelsea	0
06-11-2005	English Premier	Man Utd	1–0	Chelsea	0
12-11-2005	International	Argentina	2–3	England	0 Yellow Card
19-11-2005	English Premier	Chelsea	3–0	Newcastle	0 Yellow Card
23-11-2005	European Cup	Anderlecht	0–2	Chelsea	0
26-11-2005	English Premier	Portsmouth	0–2	Chelsea	1
03-12-2005	English Premier	Chelsea	1–0	Middlesbro	0
06-12-2005	European Cup	Chelsea	0–0	Liverpool	0 Yellow Card

10-12-2005	English Premier	Chelsea	1-0	Wigan	0
18-12-2005	English Premier	Arsenal	0-2	Chelsea	0 Yellow Card
26-12-2005	English Premier	Chelsea	3-2	Fulham	1
31-12-2005	English Premier	Chelsea	2-0	Birmingham	0
02-01-2006	English Premier	West Ham	1-3	Chelsea	1 Yellow Card
15-01-2006	English Premier	Sunderland	1-2	Chelsea	0
22-01-2006	English Premier	Chelsea	1-1	Charlton	0
28-01-2006	English FA Cup	Everton	1-1	Chelsea	1
01-02-2006	English Premier	Aston Villa	1-1	Chelsea	0
05-02-2006	English Premier	Chelsea	2-0	Liverpool	0
08-02-2006	English FA Cup	Chelsea	4-1	Everton	1
11-02-2006	English Premier	Middlesbro	3-0	Chelsea	0
19-02-2006	English FA Cup	Chelsea	3-1	Colchester	0
22-02-2006	European Cup	Chelsea	1-2	Barcelona	0
25-02-2006	English Premier	Chelsea	2-0	Portsmouth	1
07-03-2006	European Cup	Barcelona	1-1	Chelsea	1
11-03-2006	English Premier	Chelsea	2-1	Tottenham	0

19-03-2006	English Premier	Fulham	1-0	Chelsea	0
22-03-2006	English FA Cup	Chelsea	1-0	Newcastle	0
25-03-2006	English Premier	Chelsea	2-0	Man City	0

Goals: 20 Yellow Cards: 8 Red Cards: 0